TO

_____

FROM

_____

DATE

_____

BISCUITS, BUTTER AND Blessings

Farm-Fresh Devotions of Hope & Comfort

Biscuits, Butter, and Blessings:
Farm-Fresh Devotions of Hope & Comfort
Copyright © 2018 by DaySpring
First Edition, August 2018

Published by:

DaySpring

P.O. Box 1010
Siloam Springs, AR 72761
dayspring.com

Bible verses were taken from the following translations:

AMP: Scriptures taken from the Amplified® Bible, © 1954, 1958, 1962, 1964, 1965, 1987 by The Lockman Foundation. Used by permission. (www.lockman.org)

ESV: Scripture quotations taken from the ESV Bible® (The Holy Bible, English Standard Version®) copyright ©2001 by Crossway Bibles, a publishing ministry of Good News Publishers. Used by permission. All rights reserved.

HCSB: Scripture taken from the Holman Christian Standard Bible®. © 1999, 2000, 2002, 2003 by Holman Bible Publishers. Used by permission.

KJV: Scripture taken from the Holy Bible, King James Version.

The Message: Scripture quotations from The Message. © Eugene Peterson. Permission from NavPress

NASB: Scripture from the NEW AMERICAN STANDARD BIBLE ®, © Copyright 1960, 1962, 1963, 1968, 1971, 1972, 1973, 1975, 1977, 1995 by the Lockman Foundation. Used by permission. (www.lockman.org)

NIV: Scriptures marked NIV are taken from the Holy Bible, New International Version®, NIV®. Copyright © 1973, 1978, 1984, 2011 by Biblica, Inc.® Used by permission of Zondervan. All rights reserved worldwide. www.zondervan.com. The "NIV" and "New International Version" are trademarks registered in the United States Patent and Trademark Office by Biblica, Inc.®

NKJV: Scripture from the New King James Version. Copyright © 1982 by Thomas Nelson, Inc.

NLT: Scripture quotations are taken from the Holy Bible, New Living Translation, copyright © 1996, 2004, 2007 by Tyndale House Foundation. Used by permission of Tyndale House Publishers, Inc., Carol Stream, Illinois 60188. All rights reserved.

TLB: © The Living Bible. Taken from the Living Bible with permission from Tyndale House Publishers, Inc., Wheaton, IL.

Written by Linda Kozar | Designed by Jessica Wei
Typeset by Greg Jackson of thinkpen.design

Printed in China

Prime: 10972

ISBN: 978-1-68408-559-0

CONTENTS

A MESSAGE TO READERS

Because you've picked up a devotional book with the word "Biscuits" in its title, you probably have more than a passing interest in both old-time religion and down-home country wisdom. If so, you've come to the right place. On the pages that follow, you'll be treated to a collection of timeless Scripture, inspirational quotes, delightful recipes, and daily devotionals. And as you read along day by day, you'll discover a dash of down-home country humor, too.

In rural America, the Christian faith has been expressed for centuries through song and verse. Today, the gospel message remains near and dear to millions of believers who still enjoy the simple pleasures of a quiet evening spent talking and rocking on the front porch. The ideas in this book remind us that God's grace is free, that His love endures forever, and that His faithfulness extends to good ol' boys and city folk alike.

The Bible is a book like no other. It is a gift from the Creator, an instruction book for life here on Earth and a roadmap for life eternal. And it's a book of promises. When God makes a promise, He keeps it. No exceptions. So the verses in this text are not hypotheticals; they're certainties. They apply to every generation, to every nationality, and to every corner of the globe, including yours. And His promises apply to every human being, including you.

If you're ready for a heaping helping of inspiration and truth, keep reading. When you do, you'll discover that old-time religion has never gone out of style...and never will.

If Trouble Had a Baby

Ishbi-benob, who was of the sons of the giants,
the weight of whose spear was 300 shekels of bronze,
was girded with a new sword, and thought to kill David.

II SAMUEL 21:16 AMPC

Have you ever wondered why David picked up five smooth stones to fell Goliath? After years of protecting his sheep from bears and wolves, he was an expert marksman with a sling (I Samuel 17). It makes perfect sense to have more than one stone, right? Would a soldier go to war with just one bullet in the chamber? But here's another thing to consider: Goliath had four brothers, all giants like himself. Perhaps the five stones David selected were to kill not only Goliath but also his ornery, oversized brothers. As things turned out, David only had to dispatch Goliath that fateful day, but Goliath's brothers would come for David later on in life.

Problems can come up on us that way as well. You think you're done dealing with one giant problem in faith, and years later a group of oversized problems shows up snarling in your face. By the time Goliath's brothers came for David, he was older and grew faint battling them. However, David's mighty warriors, all valiant soldiers, came to his rescue and took the giants down.

FAITH CHECK

We all need help battling the giants in life. God was with David when he slew Goliath, and He was with David and his soldiers when they faced the remaining threats to his life, one by one. God does not send us out to battle giants alone. He is always with us when we face our giants and also provides prayer warriors to fight alongside us when we grow weak or faint.

There is a stone
for every giant
in your life.

He Walks with Me

*And they heard the sound of the L*ORD *God walking
in the garden in the cool of the day.*
GENESIS 3:8 ESV

Have you ever sat on a porch in the golden hour during that beautiful time before the sun dips down below the horizon? The setting sun washes a golden light over everything and everyone. And there is a hushed stillness, a sacred silence in the atmosphere, as if all of creation were holding its breath.

God the Father loved to walk and talk with Adam and Eve in the last hour of the day, when cooling breezes from the east flowed through the Garden of Eden. On one particular evening, however, Adam and Eve were no-shows, so God called out for them. Of course, He knew exactly where they were. They were hiding among the trees in the garden because they knew they had sinned, and were afraid. And to be honest, they might have been a little freaked out when they suddenly discovered they were naked. When we sin against God, that same sort of shame and fear comes over us. But instead of trying to hide our shame or walk away from God, we must remember that those who habitually walk with God may stumble at times, but they will not fall.

FAITH CHECK

Worship in the Old Testament was structured around the natural rhythm of morning and evening, to remind believers of His steadfast love in the morning and His faithfulness in the evening (Psalm 92:1–2). Perhaps we need that reminder as well.

The devil knows your name
but calls you by your sin.
God knows your sin
but calls you by your name.

Saintly Siestas

And there was a young man named Eutychus
sitting on the window sill.
ACTS 20:9 NASB

Have you ever felt yourself nodding off in church? Falling asleep in church is downright rude and embarrassing. Some people even snore! The Puritans had little patience with those given to Christian catnaps. A special usher roamed the congregation carrying a three-foot-long stick to which a green feather was attached, and he would tickle the sleeping person's nose until he or she woke up, and probably sneezed.

In the book of Acts, a young man named Eutychus fell asleep during one of the apostle Paul's long, late-night services. The trouble is, he was sitting on a window ledge and fell three stories down. Some commentators have suggested that the young man was not really dead, but Luke the physician, who was traveling with Paul, examined the young man, and it is safe to assume that the good doctor knew death when he saw it. Paul bent over the young man and embraced him, saying, "Don't be alarmed…. He's alive!" (Acts 20:10 NIV). So instead of planning a sad funeral, the congregation celebrated, and talked, and broke bread together with the young man until the sun came up.

FAITH CHECK

When Jesus was summoned by the rich ruler whose little daughter had died, He proclaimed, "Do not weep, for she is not dead but sleeping" (Luke 8:52 ESV). Jesus declared life in Lazarus though he had been dead for four days (John 11:17). No tomb could hold the little girl, or Lazarus, or Eutychus, or Jesus Himself, because Jesus is the Resurrection and the Life.

If I didn't wake up,
I'd still be sleeping.

—YOGI BERRA

The Only Wise God

From where then does wisdom come? And where is the place
of understanding? It is hidden from the eyes of all the
living, and concealed from the birds of the heavens

JOB 28:20-21 AMP

Inside the earth are beds of sapphires and the dust
of pure gold, but wisdom is nowhere to be found.
Searching for knowledge is like mining for precious
stones and minerals under the earth. Those who seek
facts and ideas must get their hands dirty as they dig
out, sift, and accumulate that knowledge. Through
research, study, investigation, observation, and experience, mankind has discovered some amazing things.
However, true wisdom is knowing what to do with
all that knowledge, and "head knowledge" won't do
anyone any good without the wisdom to know what
to do with it. Some folks are brilliant, but they can't
tell if a rail is rotten unless they sit on it. God's Word
says that the worship and reverence of the Lord is the
beginning of wisdom, and the knowledge of Him is true
understanding (Proverbs 9:10).

FAITH CHECK

So, what is wisdom? And where can understanding be
found? The answer to both questions can be found in
the Bible. "Behold, the reverential and worshipful fear
of the Lord—that is wisdom; and to depart from evil is
understanding" (Job 28:28 AMP).

Knowledge is knowing that a tomato is a fruit. Wisdom is not putting it in a fruit salad.

—MILES KINGTON

A Thorn by Any Name

To keep me from becoming conceited because of these
surpassingly great revelations, there was given me a
thorn in the flesh, a messenger of Satan to torment me.
—II CORINTHIANS 12:7 NIV

Paul traveled about preaching and teaching in more territory and with more zeal than anyone else in the New Testament—plucking souls like firebrands out of the enemy's hand and winning them to the kingdom of heaven. He was a real thorn to Satan, so why did God allow the enemy to become a thorn to Paul? Read further on in II Corinthians 12:7–9 and it is easy to see why. God saw Paul's heart. He knew that the visions and revelations given to Paul for the church would bring him notoriety, and that Paul might be tempted to boast in himself. Allowing Satan to be a thorn in Paul's flesh may have been God's way of protecting His servant from becoming conceited or prideful. Those who are full of themselves will never experience the fullness of God.

FAITH CHECK

Was Paul's thorn in the flesh a physical ailment? Or could he have been haunted by horrific memories of persecuting fellow believers? Though Paul did not share the nature of his torment, we know that God did not remove the thorn, though Paul asked Him on three separate occasions.

God sometimes uses the enemy as an instrument to refine and strengthen a believer's faith, but only within the limitations and parameters set by God Himself.

We can complain because rose bushes have thorns, or rejoice because thorn bushes have roses.

—ABRAHAM LINCOLN

Hasten to His Throne

I love the LORD, for he heard my voice; he heard
my cry for mercy. Because He turned His ear to
me, I will call on Him as long as I live.
—PSALM 116:1-2 NIV

King David wrote this psalm in gratitude to God as he ascended to the throne of Israel. Most commentators agree that he waited fifteen to twenty years from the time the prophet Samuel anointed him as a youth to the time he replaced King Saul, whom God rejected. After being relentlessly pursued and hunted down by Saul and his army, the chase was now over. On one occasion, David had the chance to take Saul's life in a cave, but he refused to slay "God's anointed," though King Saul was trying hard to kill *him*. David did not try to quicken his destiny by any other means. Instead, he lived a faithful life and waited for God's promises to be fulfilled. Have you ever been chased down relentlessly by the enemy and wondered when God would fulfill the promises He's placed in your heart?

FAITH CHECK

To live an anointed life, we must trust God to deliver us and wait in hope for His promises to come to pass in accordance with His timetable. Though the journey to his earthly throne was a long one, David always hastened to God's throne with his every fear, need, and concern. He loved the Lord with all his heart. God called David "a man after His own heart," and blessed him and his descendants forever.

Long as I live, when troubles rise, I'll hasten to His throne

—ISAAC WATTS, THE PSALMS OF DAVID

The Cactus Flower

The wilderness and the solitary place shall be glad for them; and the desert shall rejoice, and blossom as the rose.
—ISAIAH 35:1 KJV

Some plants flourish in the harshest environments. Take cactus plants for instance. They store up provisions of water and sunlight to ensure their continued existence. The curious-looking plants not only survive, they thrive. Some cactus flowers bloom once a year, some for only a night. One particular variety of cactus, the night-blooming cereus, produces a spectacular bloom. Ragged-edged, creamy opaque petals tinged with peach, gold, and green fan out into a magnificent medallion of splendor, only to fade and droop by morning. Our lives on this earth are as fleeting as those large, lovely blossoms. In view of eternity, our mortal existence flowers and fades in but a moment. But what we do with our lives in that moment is what gives our lives meaning and importance, both in the here and the hereafter.

FAITH CHECK

Like the cactus, believers must store up resources as well, specifically God's Word in our hearts to provide living water to our souls, water that will keep our souls hydrated through desert wanderings and hard times. God's Word is our provision, and a prayerful life is our decision. "Your Word I have treasured and stored in my heart, that I may not sin against You" (Psalm 119:11 AMP). Not one hopeful bloom in the desert goes unnoticed by God. He sees and appreciates the beauty of His creation and the faithfulness of those who manage to bloom to His glory, wherever they are planted.

If God brings you
to it, He will bring
you through it.

Deep Calls to Deep

Deep calls to deep in the roar of your waterfalls;
all your waves and breakers have swept over me.
—PSALM 42:7 NIV

Blue whales have the special ability to communicate with one another underwater, over vast distances. The intense haunting pulses and rhythms, deep moans, and captivating whale songs captured by sonar devices are unmistakable, though presently untranslatable. Before the 1940s, whales were able to communicate with one another at distances up to a thousand miles. However, with the introduction of modern commercial shipping and leisure boats, as well as military sonar, noise pollution in the vast oceans has sadly diminished that distance to about one hundred miles.

God the Father calls out to each of us as well through the vast gulf between us to draw us to Him, and He continues to communicate with us, as deep calls to deep, sharing His love and wisdom and care for us. Are you listening?

FAITH CHECK

As the din of modern shipping interferes with the blue whales' ability to converse with one another, the world constantly clamors for our attention as well, sending false signals that attempt to interfere with our heavenly communing. However, our ability to commune with God does not rely on sound. We respond to God's call by way of the heart, which has no limitations.

There is, one knows not what sweet mystery about this sea, whose gently awful stirrings seem to speak of some hidden soul beneath.

—HERMAN MELVILLE

Hope Full

My son, attend to my Words; incline thine ear
unto my sayings.... For they are life unto those
that find them, and health to all their flesh.
—PROVERBS 4:20–22 KJV

One day you're enjoying life, just going about your normal routine, when suddenly bad news hits you in the gut like a bazooka. Bad news is the serious kind that strikes fear into your soul, either for yourself or for someone close to you. It's the kind of news nobody wants to hear. A pregnant woman having the first ultrasound of her unborn baby is always a bit nervous. But even more so if the technician keeps zeroing in on a certain area and then suddenly stops making polite conversation. And how about when you go in for a routine exam only to have the doctor tell you they've discovered something suspicious? The tightness of fear and despair over a situation like that can be paralyzing. But we have a hope to cling to in Jesus Christ. "...For my hope is from him. He only is my rock and my salvation, my fortress; I shall not be shaken" (Psalm 62:5–6 ESV).

FAITH CHECK

God's Word is medicine to our flesh. When we speak God's Word over our situation, when we pray and immerse ourselves in scripture, when we surround ourselves with other believers who partner with us in the fight, it is impossible to lose hope, even in an impossible situation.

Faith does not operate in the realm of the possible. There is no glory for God in that which is humanly possible. Faith begins where man's power ends.

—GEORGE MUELLER

Go Fly a Kite, Canaanites!

*Yes, every pot in Jerusalem and in Judah shall be holiness
to the LORD of hosts.... In that day there shall no longer
be a Canaanite in the house of the LORD of hosts.*

— ZECHARIAH 14:21 NKJV

Why was Jesus so angry at the Canaanite money changers in the temple? A Canaanite can be described as an idolatrous Gentile or even a Jew who profanes what God calls sacred and holy, for selfish, evil, and unholy purposes. In the time of Christ, every male Israelite over twenty years of age was required to pay a half-shekel as an offering to the Lord (Exodus 30:13–15). And, let's just say that the money changer's rate of exchange was definitely in their own favor. Angered at the infestation of the Canaanite spirit in His Father's house, Jesus drove out the money changers from the temple, cleansing it from those who profaned what was sacred. Even today, there are unscrupulous people who, through artifice and fraudulent schemes, deceive others in the name of God. Such people are the true Canaanites of this age, using God's Word and free gift in profane ways.

FAITH CHECK

In God's new heaven and new earth, *every* vessel will be consecrated for use in divine service. Instead of only Levitical priests or pastors sanctified for service, every saint of God will be fit for divine service to Him. (Revelation 21:27 KJV).

Charity never
made poor,
stealing never
made rich,
and wealth never
made wise.

—ENGLISH PROVERB

Grandma's Biscuits

Perfect, yummy, flaky, and delicious biscuits. Serves 6–8.

INGREDIENTS:

- 2½ cups all-purpose flour *plus more for dusting*
- 2 tablespoons baking powder
- 1 teaspoon sugar
- 1 teaspoon salt
- 8 tablespoons cold unsalted butter
- 1 cup buttermilk
- 2 tablespoons salted butter *to brush on top*

DIRECTIONS:

- Preheat oven to 425 degrees. Sift flour, baking powder, sugar, and salt into a large mixing bowl. Cut butter into cubes *using a food processor, pastry cutter, or fork,* and add to flour, until the mixture is crumbly. Return dough to bowl, add buttermilk, and stir with a fork until it forms into a rough ball. The dough will likely be sticky.

- Turn the dough out onto a floured surface and roll gently into a rough rectangle, about one-inch thick. Fold it over and roll the dough down again. Repeat five times. Be gentle with the dough. Overworked dough equals tough biscuits.

- Gently roll the dough out some more so that it forms a rectangle. Cut dough into biscuits using a floured glass or pastry cutter. Do not twist cutter when cutting. This will crimp the edges of the biscuit and cause it not to rise. If you have scraps, reform the rectangle and cut additional biscuits.

- The secret to baking a good biscuit is to keep them friendly. With that in mind, arrange biscuits close together on a baking sheet so they're just touching, and place in oven. Bake until golden brown, approximately 10–15 minutes. Remove from oven. Brush with melted butter.

A positive attitude and a sense of humor go together like biscuits and gravy.

—DOLLY PARTON

Rise of the Dead Sea

Then he said to me, "These waters go out toward the
eastern region and go down into the Arabah; then
they go toward the sea, being made to flow into the
sea, and the waters of the sea become fresh."
— EZEKIEL 47:8–9 NASB

The Dead Sea is known by many names, but translated from Hebrew it is "The Sea of Salt." Twice as saline as the Great Salt Lake in Utah and almost ten times as salty as the oceans of the world, the Dead Sea is rich in minerals, but a poor environment for life, which makes an end-time prophecy uttered by the prophet Ezekiel startling. "And it will come about that fishermen will stand beside it.... Their fish will be according to their kinds, like the fish of the Great Sea, very many" (Ezekiel 47:10 NASB). How can this possibly happen? Though the Jordan River once infused fresh water into the Dead Sea, the flow eventually slowed to a mere trickle. However, in recent years, the situation has changed dramatically. Freshwater sinkholes have started to appear, some with live fish in them!

FAITH CHECK

The waters of the Dead Sea will one day be healed, restored, and hospitable to life. God never fails to keep His Word. Are your hopes and dreams mired in a Dead Sea of unbelief? Call out to the Source, to the true living water, who will lovingly infuse your heart and bring a new and abundant life to you.

Some of us are
like the Dead Sea,
always taking in
but never giving out,
because we are not
rightly related to
the Lord Jesus.

—OSWALD CHAMBERS

The Snake Line

But those who hope in the LORD will renew their
strength. They will soar on wings like eagles.
—ISAIAH 40:31 NIV

Early settlers believed in something called a "snake
line," a mountain elevation inhospitable to the
survival of snakes, and they were keen to build their
homes in those heights. Though the ground was rockier
and harder to farm and build upon, they considered the
higher elevations to be safer places in which to house
their families. Some campers still swear by the snake
line. They believe in pitching their tents at higher
elevations in order to avoid coming into contact with
anything slithery. However, the truth is, some snakes
can, and do, live at higher altitudes.

In this world, if you're living for Christ, no matter
where you pitch your tent in life, you will always find
yourself at odds with the enemy.

FAITH CHECK

We cannot escape the presence of the "serpent of this
world," but we can take authority over him in the name
of Jesus! Our feet are planted on this earth for a reason.
"Behold, I have given you authority to tread on serpents
and scorpions, and over all the power of the enemy, and
nothing shall hurt you" (Luke 10:19 ESV).

My favorite moments? Where it's all going swimmingly, the sun's out, and I've got a fire going and a nice snake on the barbecue.

—BEAR GRYLLS

Catnip and Kryptonite

Create in me a clean heart, O God, and renew
a right and steadfast spirit within me.
—PSALM 51:10 AMP

Euphoria for felines has a name: catnip. A true love potion for kitties, the catnip plant releases a potent oil in its leaves and stems that is known to drive felines to utter distraction. Believe it or not, catnip plants are members of the mint family. So, if cats were fond of iced tea, they would likely garnish it with a sprig of catnip!

In the Superman comics, kryptonite is the strength-draining, glow-y, green radioactive ore from his home plant of Krypton—essentially, Superman's nemesis.

But what do these two innocuous items, catnip and kryptonite, have in common? Hindrance. The enemy will either entice you with an irresistible temptation or disable you with a crippling, strength-sapping burden to keep you from fulfilling your God-given purpose in life.

FAITH CHECK

The only way the enemy's tactics can be effective in our lives is when we lose our focus on God, and instead focus in on ourselves. But we are more than conquerors through Him (Romans 8:37). Troubles will always arise on this earth, and we will always be surrounded by temptation. But the name of Jesus is our strength and shield. The enemy has a weakness too, one that he will never overcome. The name of Jesus is kryptonite to Satan! Jesus is our ultimate superhero!

We cannot give our hearts to God and keep our bodies for ourselves.

—ELISABETH ELLIOT

Balaam's Donkey

And the LORD opened the mouth of the donkey, and
she said to Balaam, "What have I done to you,
that you have struck me these three times?"
—NUMBERS 22:28–31 NASB

Balak, the king of Moab, was keen to hire a famous
soothsayer named Balaam to curse Israel so they
could drive the Israelites out of their land. But God
told Balaam, "You shall not go with them; you shall
not curse the people, for they are blessed" (Numbers
22:12 NKJV). The king kept trying to convince the
soothsayer, and Balaam kept asking God to change His
mind instead of simply obeying Him. So, God finally
told rebellious Balaam to go. Along the way, Balaam's
donkey suddenly refused to move forward, so he struck
the poor animal three times. Talk about animal cruelty!
In fact, Balaam was so mad that when the donkey started
explaining *why* he turned away, Balaam responded
without wondering how in the world a donkey could
be conversing with him. Finally, Balaam's eyes were
opened and he saw the angel of the Lord, sword drawn,
standing in his path. God used the humble, innocent
donkey to save his ungrateful master's life.

FAITH CHECK

Balaam was a pagan profiteer, not a holy prophet,
though he wound up obeying God in this instance and
blessing Israel, much to Balak's dismay. Balaam later
conspired with the Moabite king to come up with a
plan to sabotage the people of Israel to sin against God.
He was a man who kept the letter of the law but did
as he pleased. Eventually, he was slain by the sword,
discovering too late that one cannot run with the hare
and also hunt with the hounds.

The enemy cannot curse what God has blessed, but he can tempt you out of your blessings.

A Day of Rest

And Jesus said to them, The Sabbath was made on account
and for the sake of man, not man for the Sabbath.
—MARK 2:27 AMPC

As Jesus and His hungry disciples passed through a grain field, they picked heads of grain to eat along the way. Now, according to Deuteronomy 23:25, it was lawful to pick heads of grain by hand from a man's grain field, but the Pharisees demanded to know why they were "working" on the Sabbath. "Six days you shall do your work, but on the seventh day you shall rest: that your ox and your donkey may have rest, and the son of your servant woman, and the alien, may be refreshed" (Exodus 23:12 ESV). The law of Moses (Deuteronomy 5:14) commanded them to keep the Sabbath, but the question was "how" to keep it. The Jews added a burdensome number of man-made laws designed toward this end. But Jesus reminded the Pharisees that David and his men, who were also hungry in their flight from King Saul, ate the showbread, which only priests were allowed to eat. Sure, David technically broke the law of Moses, but under certain conditions of need, the violation was allowable. God created the Sabbath for humankind, as a day of rest from their toil. The Sabbath day is meant to be a blessing to us, a time of rest and restoration, and a day to worship and rejoice in the Lord, Who made us.

FAITH CHECK

"The Son of Man is lord even of the Sabbath" (Mark 2:28 ESV), but we should also be reminded that He is Lord over every day of the week.

Today, I will be
as useless as the
"G" in lasagna.

Either Near or Here

The end of all things is near; therefore, be of sound judgment and sober spirit for the purpose of prayer.
—I PETER 4:7 NASB

People used to think that ostriches actually buried their heads in the sand. And for many years, this observation was used as an analogy for those who refuse to face obvious signs of danger. The seven- to nine-foot-tall birds do appear to the naked eye as if they stick their heads in the sand, but what the birds are really doing is tending to their nests—turning their eggs with their beaks.

While the analogy is incorrect, the spirit of the saying is true. Many people ignore signs of danger in their lives because they are too busy and preoccupied to notice what's going on in the world. We're busy tending to our own nests—home, family, job, church, and entertainment and leisure activities. Warning signs might be all around us, but few will even notice or be aware. The Bible warns us about what to expect in the "last days." "For nation will rise up against nation, and kingdom against kingdom; there will be earthquakes in various places; there will be famines. These things are the beginning of the birth pangs" (Mark 13 AMP). While many people prudently prepare for emergency situations by storing up food, water, medicine, and other supplies, the most important and often neglected preparation is literally under our noses. Our hearts.

FAITH CHECK

We must nourish our hearts with God's Word daily, take time to refresh our spirits with His Living Water, and share the love of Christ in every thought, action, and deed.

We are living
on the brink
of the apocalypse,
but the world
is asleep.

—JOEL C. ROSENBERG

Son-Followers

Repent, then, and turn to God so that your sins may be wiped
out, that times of refreshing may come from the LORD.
—ACTS 3:19 NIV

Young sunflowers track the sun over the course of
a day, moving their big beautiful yellow blooms to
face the dazzling splendor of the light from east to west.
The sun-centric bloom's behavior can be explained
by circadian rhythms, behavioral changes following
a twenty-four-hour cycle. Once sunflowers reach
maturity, however, they stop tracking the sun and
permanently turn their blooms toward the east. Psalm
103:12 NKJV tells us, "As far as the east is from the
west, so far has He [Jesus] removed our transgressions
from us" (NKJV). If you were to travel upward from
the South Pole as far as you could go, a compass would
register that you were traveling north, in the direction
of the North Pole. But if the starting point of your
travel began from east to west, you would continue to
travel in an eastward direction indefinitely! Our sins
are forever forgiven, and as far as the east is from the
west, there will never be a point in time when we will
ever meet up with our sins again.

FAITH CHECK

When they mature, sunflowers turn toward the east,
where the sun rises. Like sunflowers, Son-followers
turn their hope and expectation toward the east as
well, waiting with eager hope and expectation for the
return of the Messiah. For at the end of the age, Jesus
will return "as the lightning comes from the east and
flashes to the west" (Matthew 24:27 NKJV).

Keep your face to the sunshine and you cannot see the shadows. It's what the sunflowers do.

—HELEN KELLER

Service with a Smile

And to know the love of Christ which surpasses knowledge,
that you may be filled up to all the fullness of God
— EPHESIANS 3:19 NASB

Many Baby Boomers remember when businesses used to give away quality items with their products. Oatmeal boxes contained collectible "milk glass" cups and saucers, or tiny bowls. Gas stations gave away punch bowls, dishes, silverware, or fun toys for the kids every time a customer told the attendant to "fill 'er up." An enterprising company, Sperry and Hutchinson, better known as S&H Green Stamps, came up with the idea to offer a rewards catalog in which consumers would receive trading stamps with purchases at grocery checkouts and other retail outlets to collect and later trade in for various items. If that wasn't enough, customers were treated to "Service with a Smile," and "The Customer Is Always Right," both of which have become industry standards today.

Although businesses claim "the customer is always right" here on earth, people are far from right, compared to God's standard of righteousness.

FAITH CHECK

We cannot collect our good works and trade them in like green stamps for eternal salvation. But when we repent of our sins and ask Jesus to fill our hearts, He rewards us with far more than a punch bowl, far more than all our good works could or would ever add up to. Jesus gives us the free gift of eternal salvation and forgiveness. That should put a smile on your face!

Salvation is a free gift that can only be received, never achieved.

Dry Bones

And as I prophesied, there was a sound, and behold, a
rattling, and the bones came together, bone to its bone.
—EZEKIEL 37:7 ESV

God took the prophet Ezekiel on a tour through a
valley of human bones, bones bleached white and
dry in the blazing sun. And God asked him, "Son of
man, can these bones live?" Now most of us would
have answered, "No way! These people are super dead,
and Father God, if You don't mind me saying so, this
conversation is starting to creep me out a little." But
Ezekiel trusted God, so God asked him to prophesy life
into the bones. He did, and the bones started coming
together, and muscles and sinews and flesh knit across
the skeletons. However, there was no breath in them.
So God asked Ezekiel to prophesy again, to say to the
breath, "Come from the four winds, O breath, and
breathe on these slain, that they may live" (Ezekiel
37:9 ESV). And the people came to life and rose to their
feet. Ezekiel described their number as "an exceedingly
great army."

FAITH CHECK

Have you ever felt as if the world has scorched or
gnawed off every iota of your hope and faith, and there's
nothing left but a pile of dry bones dragging itself to
church every Sunday? If God can raise the dead from
their graves, He can most certainly raise you from your
discouragements. God can replace what has wasted
away, renew your hope, and breathe new life into you.

Our faith honors
God, and in return,
God honors
our faith.

Whether You Weep or Groan

Say this to him: The LORD speaks thus: Behold, what
I have built I will break down, and that which I have
planted I will pluck up—and this means the whole land.
—JEREMIAH 45:4 AMPC

Baruch, the faithful scribe of the prophet Jeremiah,
did not always have the purest of intentions in
aligning himself with "the weeping prophet." The
prophet Jeremiah earned that title by continually
weeping before God on behalf of his people, pleading
with God to spare them from the dreadful judgments
that were to come, judgments his people had brought
upon themselves for their stubborn refusal to give up
their idolatries. Baruch, who was born into a prominent
family, saw the man of God soaring to greatness. In
serving the prophet, he hoped to share the prophet's
recognition. Instead of fame, however, Baruch shared
in Jeremiah's emotional pain and distress, which is the
true state of those to whom God has given a heart to
prophesy to His people.

Sometimes we make the same mistake as Baruch.
We seek and strive to make a name for ourselves on
this earth instead of simply *doing* what our Father
in heaven has called us to do and rejoicing in God's
promise of eternal life.

FAITH CHECK
Baruch was only thinking about his personal ambitions.
"Do you seek great things for yourself?" (Jeremiah 45:5
ESV). Though God broke the news to Baruch that he
would not have the fame or recognition he sought,
He promised to protect and preserve the scribe's life
wherever he went—a far better blessing considering
the dangerous situations the two were always in.

In the family register of glory, the small and the great are written with the same pen.

—CHARLES SPURGEON

The Good Fight

Many are saying of me, "God will not deliver
him." But You, LORD, are a shield around me, my
glory, the One who lifts my head high.
—PSALM 3:2-3 NIV

Whatever trial or situation you find yourself in, and
you're suddenly facing the fight of your life, it's
important to ask others to join with you in the battle.
When the Israelites battled the Amalekites, Joshua
succeeded against the enemy when Moses held his
arms up. But as the battle raged, Moses grew tired.
Try holding your arms up for an entire day! When
he lowered his arms, the Israelites started losing, so
Aaron and Hur figured out that if Israel was going to
win this battle they were going to have to help Moses
keep his arms up (Exodus 17:12).

When your life is on the line, and you don't have the
strength on your own to pray, or praise, or keep your
faith up, that's when praying friends need to come to
your rescue.

FAITH CHECK

Ask everyone to pray, but know that only a few faithful prayer warriors will truly pray you through each
step of your circumstance. A promise made with the
purest intention is not always intentionally followed
through. Appeal to believers who have the gift of
encouragement. Ask them to periodically remind you
what God's Word has to say about your situation.
Remember, the faithful few will your faith renew!

Whoever refreshes
others will himself
be refreshed.

—PROVERBS 11:25 NIV

Apples of Gold

A word spoken at the right time is like gold apples
on a silver tray. A wise correction to a receptive
ear is like a gold ring or an ornament of gold.
—PROVERBS 25:11-12 HCSB

Has someone ever said the perfect thing to you at
the perfect time? When you are going through an
emotional time, when your heart is in distress, the right
words can truly be precious to your troubled heart.
The Scripture above is derived from a lovely visual of
golden fruit in a silver filigree, or lattice-style basket,
which reveals the contrasting golden color of the fruit
inside. The fruit in the metal basket might be golden
apples, oranges, pomegranates, citrons, or apricots.
The apples of gold are the fruit within the basket, and
the basket is the setting of silver containing the fruit.
The delicious fruit and the gleaming, polished basket
are truly lovely together.

FAITH CHECK

The gospel of Jesus Christ is "the perfect fruit,"
appealing to our weary souls (Isaiah 50:4) and
spoken in the right season of our lives. This beautiful
message is God's Word, fitly spoken, giving peace and
redemption to weary travelers who find no rest in this
world. God's truth releases us from the chains of sin
and cradles us in His grace. The apples of gold we
share with others are scripture verses that set us free
and calm our hearts, wrapped in a setting of silver,
which is God's grace embracing us as we speak with
all humility and love.

Sometimes the right word spoken at the right time fits just right, into an empty place in your heart.

Bona Fide

He who sows the good seed is the Son of Man.
The field is the world, the good seeds are the sons of the
kingdom, but the tares are the sons of the wicked one.
—MATTHEW 13: 36–40 NKJV

Ever heard the phrase *"bona fide"*? It's Latin for "in good faith," or "without fraud," which is a sincere, honest intention or belief, regardless of the outcome of an action. If a used car salesman were to tell you, "This Chrysler Cordoba has bona fide, fine 'Corinthian leather' seats," his words are deceptive, because there is no such thing. The term was an advertising gimmick back in the seventies.

In the Bible, Christ talks about real and false believers, comparing them to wheat and tares. Farmers were aware that attempting to remove tares, which resemble wheat, could result in accidentally uprooting the wheat as well. Tares, also known as *darnel*, are only revealed at the time of harvest, when the brown ear of the wheat plant appears. The ear of the tare is black. "The enemy who sows them [tares] is the devil. The harvest is the end of the age, and the harvesters are angels" (Matthew 13:35–43 NIV).

FAITH CHECK

When man tries to play God and take on His task of separating true believers from false believers, certain disaster results. We must trust God's decision to leave the tares with the wheat until the end of the age, when Jesus returns to harvest the souls of the righteous.

The year goes wrong, and tares grown strong, hope starves without a crumb; but God's time is our harvest time. And that is sure to come.

—LEWIS J. BATES

Shadows Cast

What is the sign that the LORD will heal me?
—II KINGS 20:8 HCSB

King Hezekiah was extremely sick. The prophet Isaiah came in and gave the king a message from God, telling him "to put his house in order," because he was going to die. The prophet may not have had the best bedside manner, but hearing those words did something to the king's heart. He turned his face to the wall and cried out in repentance. So, God sent Isaiah back with the message that because Hezekiah had repented, God was going to heal him and give him fifteen more years of life. Now, for most people, that message would be enough, but not for Hezekiah. He asked the Lord for a sign that He would heal him. So, the prophet Isaiah asked him if he wanted the Lord to move the shadow on the sundial forward ten degrees or back by ten degrees. Hezekiah chose the latter because he assumed that going against nature, moving time backward, would be a greater sign. The shadow of death was upon King Hezekiah, but God moved heaven and earth because he repented.

FAITH CHECK

The poet Robert Louis Stevenson wrote in "My Shadow", "I have a little shadow that goes in and out with me, and what can be the use of him is more than I can see." When the sun is high in the sky, your shadow is short and compact. When the sun is lower in the sky, your shadow is long and thin. Whether you are rich or poor, king or citizen "Whoever dwells in the shelter of the Most High, will rest in the shadow of the Almighty" (Psalm 91:1 NIV).

*Time flies
over us,
but leaves
its shadow
behind.*

—NATHANIEL HAWTHORNE

The Tooth and Nothing but the Tooth

Like a bad tooth and an unsteady foot is confidence
in a faithless man in time of trouble.
—PROVERBS 25:19 NASB

Some people have what are called "summer" teeth: some are here, some are there. One thing is certain, an aching tooth will get your undivided attention, no matter how busy you are. The Bible compares this throbbing pain to an unfaithful friend. Have you ever turned to a person you believed to be your friend in a time of trouble and been disappointed? There's no pain like that. It is often said that prosperity brings friends, while adversity tests them. A true friend will help you through tough situations or circumstances. A true friend can be trusted to keep what you say private. A true friend is there for you when you truly need them. But no matter how good a real friend can be, eventually that person will fail you, often through no fault of their own. We're only human, as they say. To place our trust in man instead of God is the biggest mistake any of us can make. God alone is worthy of our complete trust and confidence.

FAITH CHECK

Too many people today have straight teeth and crooked morals. Trust in God and take your problems to Him first. And if you have good friends, thank Him for blessing you with them. A true friend is precious and rare. Hang onto good friends like you hang onto your teeth.

Be true to your teeth or they will be false to you.

Five Biscuit Butters to Make Your Life Better

What could make soft, flakey biscuits even better? Sweet, tangy flavored butters, of course!

Lemon Butter

INGREDIENTS:

- 1 teaspoon lemon zest
- Juice from one lemon
- 2 tablespoons lemon curd
- ¼ cup powdered sugar
- ½ cup (one stick) butter

DIRECTIONS:

1. Cream powdered sugar and softed butter together. Add the remaining ingredients and mix together until smooth.

2. Place mixture in refrigerator in a little jar or storage container with a lid. Yields one-fourth cup.

Whipped Honey Butter

INGREDIENTS:

- ½ cup softened butter
- ½ teaspoon vanilla
- ½ cup honey

DIRECTIONS:

1. Whip softened butter with an electric mixer until light and fluffy.
2. Drizzle in vanilla and honey gradually.
3. Beat again until mixture is light and fluffy. Store in the refrigerator in a little jar with a lid.

Strawberry Honey Butter

INGREDIENTS:

- 1 pint strawberries
- 1½ sticks butter
- 3 tablespoons honey
- 2 teaspoons lemon juice

DIRECTIONS:

1. Puree strawberries in a food processor. Then, strain strawberry puree through a strainer and into a medium-sized pot.
2. Add honey and lemon juice while bringing mixture to a boil. Continue boiling for three minutes, stirring constantly until mixture thickens slightly.
3. Cool to room temperature.
4. Once cooled, mix with a hand mixer, cooled strawberry mixture and the softened butter. Store in refrigerator in a little jar with a lid. Serves 12.

Brown Sugar Cinnamon Honey Butter

INGREDIENTS:

- 1 tablespoon honey
- ½ cup salted butter (one stick)
- ¼ cup dark brown sugar
- 1 teaspoon ground cinnamon

DIRECTIONS:

1. Mix all ingredients together.
2. Store in refrigerator in a little jar with a lid.

Better-than-Grannie's Apple Butter

INGREDIENTS:

- 5 pounds Gala apples
- 1 cup brown sugar packed light
- 1 cinnamon stick
- ½ teaspoon salt

DIRECTIONS:

1. Peel, core and slice apples. Grate apples in batches. Place in slow-cooker. Add remaining ingredients.
2. Cook on high setting for four hours.
3. Remove cinnamon stick and set aside. Puree apple mixture. Return to slow cooker with cinnamon stick.
4. Cook uncovered on high for four more hours, stirring occasionally.
5. Remove and discard cinnamon stick. Cool mixture completely. Transfer apple butter to jars, seal tightly and store in refrigerator for up to 3 weeks.

Fine words butter no parsnips.

—DANISH PROVERB

All the Tea in China

You shall not test the LORD Your God.
—MATTHEW 4:7 AMP

Have you ever heard somebody say, "Not for all the tea in China"? The saying stems from the fact that China produces tea in mass quantities, about a quarter of the world's supply. So, to say no to something, even if offered "all the tea in China," means nothing is going to change your mind no matter what incentives are offered.

Jesus was led by the Holy Spirit into the wilderness to be tempted by the devil. The devil took Jesus up on a very high mountain and showed Him all the kingdoms of the world, saying, "All these things I will give You, if You will fall down and worship me" (Matthew 4:9 AMP). Now if any of us could imagine ourselves in Jesus's sandals, we'd want to give that old devil the stank eye and tell him he had a lot of nerve offering us our Father's own stuff. But Jesus, the Son of God, answered him the righteous way, with Scripture. "Go away, Satan! For it is written and forever remains written, 'You shall worship the Lord your God, and serve Him only'" (Matthew 4:10 AMP).

FAITH CHECK

The devil is always about the business of tempting us away from God's promises. He tries to woo us away with money and luxury, power, fame, and pleasures— none of which hold eternal worth. Store up treasures in heaven instead, with Godly love, acts of kindness, humility, and sacrifice. And when that old serpent comes around to tempt you, just turn your face away and say, "Not for all the tea in China!"

I always fear that creation will expire before tea time.

—REV. SYDNEY SMITH

Abraham's Ceiling

And the LORD brought Abram outside [his tent into
the night] and said, "Look now toward the heavens and
count the stars—if you are able to count them."
—GENESIS 15:5 AMP

Most times when we pray, we look up at the ceiling. And some of us begin to believe that's where God is! Abram was in his tent one evening with Sarai, his wife, when God called him outside and told him to look up at the starlight. God told him to count the stars. *One one-thousand, two one-thousand, three one-thousand.* Who knows when Abram quit counting? But God had made His point. Abram's descendants would be more numerous than the stars in the heavens. At seventy-five years old, Abram was not exactly in the prime of life. And Sarai's eggs were way past the expiration date. How was this going to happen? Abram and Sarai did what a lot of people do today. They got tired of waiting on God to fulfill His promise and figured out a way to fulfill God's promise on their own with Hagar, Sarah's handmaiden. We all know how that worked out. Do-it-yourself faith is a downright disaster.

FAITH CHECK

God called Abram out of his tent to talk to him that night because He wanted him to see what big dreams look like. Abram wanted a child, yet God gave him innumerable children. God's dreams are so big, they cannot be contained in the confines of a tent or by the smallness of our own plans or desires. He has a plan and a purpose for your life that is bigger than you could ever imagine. And God won't give you anything until He gives you everything.

*Dreams come a size
too big so we can
grow into them.*

His Story

Looking unto Jesus the author and finisher of
our faith; who for the joy that was set before Him
endured the cross, despising the shame, and is set
down at the right hand of the throne of God.
—HEBREWS 12:2 KJV

If you love books, it's safe to say that your eyes are
likely glued to the pages of your latest-greatest read.
You get lost in the book every spare moment you can
get. Some say that reading is like dreaming with open
eyes, and like dreams, there are stories with more
twists than a pretzel factory! Books take us on wild
adventures to mysterious or exotic places. Stories whisk
us back in time or propel us to a fantastical future.
Books often take readers right to the doorstep of the
most interesting people we could ever hope to meet.

What about your story? Everyone has a life story to
tell. True, God is the author and finisher of our faith,
but everything that happens each moment from the
day you were born, right until the very end, is up to
you. The course of your life is not set in earthly stone.
God has a purpose and calling for each of us, but He
allows us the opportunity to choose to follow Him in
faith or go our own way.

FAITH CHECK

An angry Moses broke into pieces the first Tablets of
Testimony on which the Ten Commandments were in-
scribed (Exodus 32:19). But God later replaced them. If
your life is shattered, remember that our Father joyfully
edits the life stories of those who repent, giving each a
clean slate to a "right" life. "God authors desires in your
heart, then fulfills His will by enabling you to realize
those desires" (Edwin Louis Cole).

My workout
is reading
in bed until
my arms hurt.

Heaven Bound

He has made my mouth like a sharp sword, in the shadow of His hand He has concealed me; and He has also made me a select arrow, He has hidden me in His quiver.

— ISAIAH 49:2 NASB

Henry Wadsworth Longfellow wrote a poem that began with this line: "I shot an arrow into the air. It fell to earth, I knew not where." These days, a guy could get arrested for something like that. What if someone else wrote the next line? "In my foot, that's where! Your arrow landed in my foot, you reckless fool! Who shoots a stray arrow into the air? You'll be hearing from my attorney." Pulling an arrow back against a bow involves stretching and pulling back, tautness and a heightened sense of expectation—an expectation that prepares you for the launch into flight that is about to happen. Our faith is a lot like that. The expectation is our faith. In Latin the phrase, *ad maiora* means "towards greater things." The expression is a favorable wish, a blessing you speak into someone's life. God has many blessings for your life. Trust Him, even when you feel like you're either going nowhere or being held back. His desire for you is to go forward towards those greater things.

FAITH CHECK

Remember, you have to pull an arrow backwards on the bowstring in order to launch it forward. When circumstances seem to be pulling you backwards, get ready. God is fixing to launch you!

Expectancy is the atmosphere of miracles.

—EDWIN LOUIS COLE

Captain Fudge

Do not swear falsely by My name and so profane
the name of your God. I am the LORD.
—LEVITICUS 19:12 NIV

Captain Fudge is not the brand-name of some kind of yummy chocolate cookie, nor is it a metaphor for a person suffering from acute food poisoning. "Lying Fudge," as he was nicknamed, was a seventeenth-century salty seafarer with a tendency to fib a lot. Fudge regularly twisted the truth and slacked off on his captain-ly duties on the ship, so much so that Isaac D'Israeli, father of the statesman Benjamin D'Israeli, quoted a story in *Curiousities of Literature, 1791,* suggesting that Captain Fudge "always brought home his owners a good cargo of lies." Is there a Captain Fudge in your life? We all seem to know someone who "lies like a Persian rug."

FAITH CHECK

When someone "fudges" an explanation or a story with malicious intent to deceive, that person has put together a fictional account of something that happened but with a different outcome, or something that didn't happen at all. We must be aware of and ever careful to represent our Father in heaven and not the "father of lies" (John 8:44 ESV). Believers bear the banner of God's truth with them wherever they go. Living God's truth is just as important as sharing God's truth.

But he that sows lies in
the end shall not lack
of a harvest, and soon
he may rest from toil
indeed, while others reap
and sow in his stead.

—J.R.R. TOLKIEN

Gold in Them Thar Trees

For by one Spirit are we all baptized into one body,
whether we be Jews or Gentiles, whether we be bond
or free; and have been all made to drink into one
Spirit. For the body is not one member, but many.
— I CORINTHIANS 12:13-14 KJV

Quaking aspen trees thrive in northern climates and are known for their beautiful, tall trunks with smooth, pale bark marked by black scarring. Their leaves are green and glossy but in autumn are golden or brilliant yellow. Due to the manner in which the heart-shaped leaves are attached to the flattened stems, the slightest breeze trembles and shakes the golden leaves, transforming a stand of aspens into a beautiful, quivering display of gold. Each aspen in a grove is a clone of the other, and the stand of trees together is considered to be one organism because new trees sprout from a common root system. In a similar way, believers are rooted in the Holy Spirit and connected to one another, though that connection is not visible to the natural sight, just as underground roots are not visible to the eye.

FAITH CHECK

A tree's roots won't grow deep if they can get the water easily. Trees need to fight and press hard to send their roots into the ground to tap into the deep water beneath. As believers, it is important for us to drink regularly from the living water of God, by daily reading His Word, the Bible. We all have a job to do in this life, and if we work together to "be about our Father's business," (Luke 2:49), we will thrive together in Him and achieve what God has called us to do. A beautiful sight indeed.

Nature is the art of God.

—DANTE

Tales from the Outhouse

And you, take wheat and barley, beans and lentils,
millet and emmer, and put them into a single vessel and
make your bread from them.... And you shall eat it as a
barley cake, baking it in their sight on human dung.
—EZEKIEL 4:9, 12 ESV

The prophet Ezekiel was always quick to obey the Lord's commands, but when God told him to bake his bread on top of human dung, it is likely he did a double take. Why would God command such a thing? The answer: to illustrate to the sinful idol-worshipping nation of Israel that they would be defiled in many more ways living as captives among foreign nations. Baking bread over dung was symbolic of defilement. That's a concept most folks across both Old and New Testament times have no problem understanding. The Lord spoke through His holy prophets to chasten and warn His chosen people to turn away from unrighteousness. Although the Lord's anger was kindled against them, it is important to point out that He never stopped loving Israel. God loves us as well with that same fierce love, a love that is unwilling to give up on us even when we sin and turn our backs to Him.

FAITH CHECK

Ezekiel reminded God that he had never defiled himself by eating unclean things, and it's not hard to imagine that he probably held his breath, anxious for God to respond. Thankfully, God relented and allowed the prophet to cook with cow dung instead. Still not very appealing, but definitely the lesser of two evils.

Everyone knows that the length of a minute depends on what side of the bathroom door you're on.

Au Lait!

For this reason He says, "Awake, sleeper, and
rise from the dead, and Christ will shine [as
dawn] upon you and give you light."
—EPHESIANS 5:14 AMP

Coffee drinkers think of their favorite beverage like a
warm fireplace for the soul. But people in Louisiana
take their obsession to a different level, with coffee
so strong it can almost hold a spoon up on its own. If
you've ever visited the city, you have no doubt sampled
a strong cup of café au lait, made with steamed milk
and "coffee and chicory." So, what is the stuff? Chicory
is a woody, perennial plant that is part of the dandelion
family. The addition of the root to coffee originated
as a coffee substitute in France during Napoleon's
Continental Blockade of 1808 and later in places like
Louisiana, with heavy French cultural influence.
But chicory gained even more popularity during the
American Civil War, when coffee again became scarce
due to blockades and trade disruption. After the war
ended, people were so accustomed to the taste of coffee
and chicory, they decided they couldn't do without it.

FAITH CHECK

Sometimes you can't get what you think you need or
want out of life, and God gives you something else. You
may not think too much of the substitution at the time,
but instead of complaining about your situation, take
what God offers you with a thankful heart. You may
not be glad you did today, or tomorrow, but one day you
might feel like you just can't do without it.

I have measured out my life with coffee spoons.

—T.S. ELIOT

Running the Race

Do you not know that in a race all the runners run, but only one receives the prize? So run that you may obtain it.
—I CORINTHIANS 9:24 ESV

They say nobody ever drowned in sweat. Try telling that to a runner after a marathon! Whether competing in a 5K or a marathon, every runner wants to cross the finish line before everybody else. The apostle Paul compared competitive runners to believers, running a spiritual race. The difference is that all who finish running "the good race" are victorious winners, who all receive a crown of righteousness. But not all who run will finish. There are those who have good intentions to run the race but cannot get going because they fail to lay aside every weight and sin. And there are others who try to run in their natural strength and abilities but are soon exhausted. Believers must rely on God to help them run with patience, endurance, and perseverance against the difficulties and temptations that lie in their path, laying aside every worldly weight and burden.

FAITH CHECK

No one runs a race by looking backward. Runners face forward, as they propel themselves toward their destination, the finish line. A believer's destination is heaven. Look toward Jesus as you run your race. And as you cross the finish line, to the cheers of a great cloud of witnesses (Hebrews 12:1), the true celebration begins!

I never run with scissors. Those last two words were unnecessary.

Lemuel's Mama

If you can find a truly good wife,
she is worth more than precious gems!
— PROVERBS 31:10 TLB

Behind every great man is a great woman, and Lemuel, king of Massa, had a great mother. The name Lemuel means "for God," or "devoted to God." Lemuel is attributed as the author of the famous Proverbs 31 passage about the virtuous woman. However, many scholars believe that King Solomon is the true author and the name Lemuel is merely his mother, Bathsheba's, pet name for him. The introduction to the proverb states, "These are the wise sayings of King Lemuel...taught to him at his mother's knee" (Proverbs 31:1 TLB). Whoever Lemuel and his mother were, the woman gave him some wise and wonderful advice indeed. Don't fall into the trap of immorality. Don't drink too much. Stand up for people. Be a good man. Hers is the kind of advice your own mother might have given you.

FAITH CHECK
Although King Solomon started off his reign well, he eventually married seven hundred wives and acquired three hundred concubines, many of whom wooed him away from God to worship idols. If Solomon and Lemuel are one and the same, his life is a lesson on why one should follow good Godly counsel. Advice won't do you any good if you don't follow it. As the saying goes, if you can't be a good example to others, then be a terrible warning to them.

If at first you don't succeed, do it the way your mother told you to.

Fixin' To

Watch therefore, for you know neither the day nor the hour.
—MATTHEW 25:13 ESV

There's a funny bumper sticker that's been around for years: "Jesus is coming. Look busy." The saying was probably written to remind us, via a smile, of all the slackers in the world who truly aren't busy going about their Father's business. Ask a slacker to pick up a broom and sweep a room, and all they ever wind up doing is pushing dirt around aimlessly. There are many believers who behave in a similar fashion, trying hard to look busy, volunteering lots of their time, and giving of their many resources. They receive recognition, accolades, and awards yet accomplish next to nothing to further God's kingdom. Instead of writing our own list of what to do for God, or allowing someone else to fill it in, why not ask God to provide you with His list? It is far better to accomplish one thing God has called you to do than ten things man asks you to do.

FAITH CHECK

"Fixing to" is a Southern colloquialism that means "to get ready, put in order, make tidy, and prepare." When someone tells you they're fixin' to do this or that, it's going to happen for sure, but they might just take their sweet time about doing the deed. Jesus is fixin' to come back to this earth. What will He find *you* doing when He arrives?

There is absolutely
no excuse for laziness.
But if you find one,
let me know.

Guardians of the Galaxy

For He shall give His angels charge over you,
to keep you in all your ways
—PSALM 91:11 NKJV

Do each of us have an angel of God to keep a divine eye on us round-the-clock—a ministering spirit, assigned by our Father in heaven to look after the faithful, to protect, guide, encourage, and comfort us? Scripture does mention and allude to this very thing. "Take heed that you do not despise one of these little ones, for I say to you that in heaven their angels always see the face of My Father who is in heaven" (Matthew 18:10 NKJV). Angels have direct access to God and receive instructions from Him concerning our care. Some Bible commentators believe we have more than one angel assigned to look after us. Heaven knows, some of us certainly seem to need a lot more protection!

FAITH CHECK

Angels are supernatural beings created by God. When we die, we do not become angels, nor do angels transform into human beings. We are not to worship or regard angels as gods, but they are God's holy messengers, who represent His eternal will and purpose. Only God knows our thoughts, and His angels act in accordance with God the Father's instructions concerning our every need or situation.

The reason angels can fly is because they take themselves lightly.

—G.K. CHESTERTON

Executive Pardon

If we confess our sins, he is faithful and just to forgive us our sins, and to cleanse us from all unrighteousness.
— I JOHN 1:9 KJV

Few turkeys would consider themselves lucky, if they happened to know what luck is. The holiday tradition of pardoning turkeys can be traced back to President Abraham Lincoln in 1863. The White House tradition has continued since then, with each succeeding president pardoning one or two turkeys each year before the Thanksgiving holiday. After a bit of fanfare, the feathered friends are delivered to "Gobbler's Rest," an area set aside at Virginia Tech's College of Agriculture and Life Sciences, to live out their lives far, far away from the dinner table. But sadly, most of the beautiful "jailbirds" gobble their last within months of arriving. It seems that turkeys raised in captivity are bred to be eaten, which means they're incredibly overweight. In fact, most of the birds are so fat that their heart and other organs can't handle the strain of living.

FAITH CHECK

Farm-raised turkeys are born to die, but so are we. Born into sin, we are all condemned to spiritual and eternal death, but the good news is, Jesus paid the price for us to live. The Son of God pardoned our sins by taking our place at the chopping block and dying for us. When you repent and ask Jesus into your heart, you are instantly born again, and will spend eternity with Him in heaven. And you can best believe, heaven's a whole lot swankier than Gobbler's Rest.

May your stuffing be tasty.
May your turkey be plump.
May your potatoes and gravy
have nary a lump. May your
yams be delicious, and your
pies take the prize. And may
your Thanksgiving dinner
stay off of your thighs.

—GRANDPA JONES

Cheese Grits

INGREDIENTS:

- 6 cups water
- 2¼ teaspoons salt
- 2 cups yellow grits *not instant*
- 1 stick unsalted butter
- ½ teaspoon black pepper
- ½ pound grated cheddar cheese
- 3 large eggs
- 1 cup milk
- Bacon crumbles, *prepared ahead of time*

DIRECTIONS:

1. Preheat oven to 350 degrees.

2. Fill a 4-quart pot with water and bring to a boil. Add salt.

3. Sprinkle grits slow and steady, stirring constantly. Reduce heat to low and simmer, stirring frequently so grits won't stick to the sides or the bottom of the pan until the mixture thickens.

4. Add butter, 1½ teaspoons salt, pepper, and cheese. Stir together until butter and cheese are melted. Lightly beat eggs and milk in a small bowl, then combine with grits mixture.

5. Pour into lightly-greased 8-inch square baking dish and bake for one hour, or until lightly browned and set.

6. Garnish with bacon crumbles and additional grated cheddar as desired. Serves eight.

*True grits,
more grits, fish,
grits, and collards.
Life is good
where grits are
"swallered".*

—ROY BLOUNT, JR.

Sips and Gossips

Do not let any unwholesome talk come out of your mouths,
but only what is helpful for building others up according
to their needs, that it may benefit those who listen.
—EPHESIANS 4:29 NIV

Women always seem to be the object of finger-pointing when it comes to gossiping. However, it's a well-known but oft-hidden fact that men like to share tasty tidbits too. Sure, some women like to spill the tea about other people, but men seem to dish the dirt out differently. Men prefer to gather in small groups to shoot the breeze about the news, old friends from school, good-looking women, salaries, their bosses, or their status. They will make fun of one another directly to the other person's face. Thinning hair or a spare tire around the stomach is cause for mutual laughs. But women would never dream of confronting someone about the way they look. Instead, they whisper to each other about such things on the sly. Both men and women love to share a spicy bit of scandal, but regardless of gender or the reason for telling tales and talking trash about one another, gossiping is wrong.

FAITH CHECK

A gossiper is someone who has or believes they have private or privileged information about someone or a situation and reveals that information to others. Whether you've been the subject of gossip or have babbled about someone else, the fruit of slanderous words results in broken trust, hurt feelings, and sometimes even disastrous consequences.

If you ran like your mouth, you'd be in good shape.

King of the Wild Frontier

But the thing David had done displeased the LORD.
—II SAMUEL 11:27 NIV

Born in a log cabin on the banks of the Nolichucky River in Tennessee, Davy Crockett became a hero, frontiersman, soldier, and politician, and is commonly referred to as the "King of the Wild Frontier." The tall tales in American folklore claim that Davy climbed Niagara Falls on an alligator's back and single-handedly wrung the tail off Halley's Comet.

God's biography about each of us is quite different from our own, however. God allowed King David's life story to be an open book, revealing him to be a man of great faith, and great sin. What would you do if God amended the Bible to include your life story? We would likely all be ashamed and embarrassed. However, when we repent and ask forgiveness, God changes our story and completely erases our sins. He compares this forgiveness to casting our sins to the bottom of the sea (Micah 7:19).

FAITH CHECK

Davy Crockett died with hundreds of other brave men on March 6, 1836, defending the Alamo at San Antonio de Béxar in the Texas Revolution. A television series depicting his adventures premiered in the sixties, starring popular actor Fess Parker in a coonskin cap, and was wildly successful.

Worry about your character and not your reputation. Because your character is who you are, and your reputation is only what people think of you.

All-Consuming Fire

And if the righteous scarcely be saved,
where shall the ungodly and the sinner appear?
— I PETER 4:18 KJV

Thanks to God's law of reaping and sowing, we don't have to wait until we get to heaven to enjoy a portion of the good we've sown here on earth. But God chastises and corrects us for our sins as well, which He is right to do as a loving Father. If a believer robs a bank, there's no exemption—no get-out-of-jail free card. Now, since judgment begins in the house of God, with the righteous, we know that the end of the wicked will be very bad. It is far better for us that God corrects our behavior here on earth, so that we can get back on course living a righteous life in Christ. Sin is a rival to righteousness. "The LORD your God is a consuming fire, a jealous God" (Deuteronomy 4:24 NIV). Even Moses, the most honored of the Old Testament saints, was chastised by God for sinning (Numbers 20:8). The faithful servant who first saw God as a burning bush on a mountaintop was not allowed to set foot in the beautiful Promised Land.

FAITH CHECK
"Some work for this world, which we do see, and God gives them what they earn in this life; some work for the world above, which we cannot see, and God gives them what they will earn in this life forever and ever likewise" —C. Kingsley, *All Saint's Day and Other Sermons,* p.265.

Sin is still sin, no matter how you spell it.

—EDWIN LOUIS COLE

Before a Fall

*He will wad you up in His hands like a ball and toss
you away into a distant, barren land; there you will
die, O glorious one—you who disgrace your nation!*
— ISAIAH 22:18 TLB

Shebna was the chief steward and scribe to King Hezekiah. He held a high and honorable office, and he knew it. But instead of giving glory to God like he should have, he sought personal glory, even commissioning a fancy tomb for himself. Shebna wanted to be remembered as a powerful and significant figure in Jerusalem's history. But Isaiah had prophesied that Judah and Jerusalem would be carried away into exile for their sins, a message from God that Shebna chose not to believe. So, God made Himself clear. Shebna would never occupy his prestigious tomb, nor be remembered in honor, but would die an inglorious death in exile. God chose another of the king's servants instead, Eliakim, the son of Hilkiah (I Kings 18:18), to fill the position. Shebna sought glory and ambition for himself and found shame, but because Eliakim's heart was turned toward God, he was given honor, position, and authority.

FAITH CHECK

We can hope for either a place among crumbling earthly tombs or a mansion among the many regal mansions in heaven. It is far better to be famous in heaven than on earth, where time weathers away a name carved into stone and the memories of great achievements fade. Those whose names are written in the Lamb's Book of Life will forever be remembered by God.

The proud person always wants to do the right thing, the great thing. But because he wants to do it in his own strength, he is fighting not with man, but with God.

—SOREN KIERKEGAARD

Just Peachy

How sweet are Your words to my taste!
Yes, sweeter than honey to my mouth!
—PSALM 119:103 NASB

If you don't live in the South, you may not be aware that Southerners speak in sugar, pouring out syrupy salutations with genuine heartfelt hospitality. Forget calling folks by their given names! Regardless of gender, if you travel south of the Mason-Dixon line, you'll soon find yourself being addressed as Honey, Darling, Sweetie, or Sugar. And if you do something nice, you might be called a Peach or a Sweet Pea. A woman might be pretty as a peach, peachy-keen, or be said to have a peaches-and-cream complexion. But if you're sluggish in the heat and humidity, someone might shake their head and say you're "slow as molasses in July." And look out if you don't return a wave or a friendly smile! You might be called a pucker-faced persimmon.

FAITH CHECK

If your Southern grandmother calls you Honey Bunch, Sweetie-Pie, Sugar Pie, or Cutie-Pie, you know beyond all doubt that you are loved. How wonderful would it be if everyone knew they were loved, and valued, and spoken to in kind endearments? Jesus loves all of us, but we are here on this earth to speak His sweetness into one another's lives. Whatever longitude and latitude you live in, try adding some Scriptural sugar to the words you speak.

If I were any
peachier, I'd be
a cobbler!

Worth the Weight

Again the Israelites cried out to the LORD, and he
gave them a deliverer—Ehud, a left-handed man,
the son of Gera the Benjamite. The Israelites
sent him with tribute to Eglon king of Moab.
—JUDGES 3:15 NIV

The Israelites rebelled against the Lord and were delivered into the hand of the king of Moab, who was a very obese man. But they repented and cried out to God, and God answered them. When it was time to deliver the yearly tribute to the king, they sent Ehud, who strapped a dagger on his right thigh under his clothing. The usual place for a dagger was on the left side so it could be rapidly drawn out by the right hand. But unlike most, Ehud was a left-handed man. He met the king in his summer parlor, and after the tribute was displayed to him, Ehud told the king he had a message from God to give to him. King Eglon eagerly dismissed his attendants and came closer to hear what Ehud had to say. But Ehud's dagger delivered a very different message than what the king expected. Ehud plunged the short dagger into the corpulent king and the handle drew in after the blade, the fat closing over it.

FAITH CHECK

Ehud escaped across an upstairs porch and mustered an army from Ephraim. They attacked and conquered the Moabites that day. Israel was at peace for the next eighty years. The only message the oppressor of God's people could hope to receive was one of judgment. God used one unlikely warrior to make a difference that day. And He can use you too. Your uniqueness is a special asset to God, not a hindrance.

I wish everything was as easy as getting fat.

The Winter House
and the Summer House

"And I shall tear down the winter house with the summer
house, and the houses of ivory shall also perish, and the man
and the great houses shall come to an end," says the LORD.

—AMOS 3:15 AMP

Kings and princes in the East loved luxury living and
decorated their multiple dwellings with all manner
of extravagance. They even inlaid their walls with
ivory, the elephant's tooth, and with precious stones
and metals. The wealthy children of Israel who dwelt
in Samaria followed the practice of owning two homes
as well, one in the city and one in the countryside. The
winter house would be positioned so that it faced the
south in order to take advantage of the sunshine, and
the summer house faced the north, to take advantage of
the cooler winds. But God warned them that He would
destroy both houses because they used their power to
steal from and oppress the poor, and crush the needy
(Amos 4:1). They thought they were storing up wealth
for themselves, but everything they possessed became
plunder for someone else to take.

FAITH CHECK

God does nothing without revealing His secret to His
servants, the prophets (Amos 3:7), to give the people an
opportunity to repent and avoid their doom. He always
warns His people of coming judgments. He warned
Noah of the coming flood, Abraham and Lot about
Sodom and Gomorrah, Joseph of the seven-year famine,
and Jonah of the coming destruction of Nineveh. If we
are quick to hear and repent of our sins, God is quick
to forgive us and will rescue us from or hold back His
judgments against us.

When people treat
you like they don't
care, believe them.

Listen Up!

Even a fool who keeps silent is considered wise;
when he closes his lips, he is deemed intelligent.
—PROVERBS 17:28 ESV

A poet once said that rain grows flowers, but all thunder does is make noise. Yet all that many people do when they're trying to prove a point is fire off a thundering of words. It is ironic that as a person raises the volume of their speech in order to be heard, the less their words are actually heard by others. Some people even resort to lashing out against individuals, but that tactic doesn't work either. Personal attacks only alienate the offender further from the people they are trying to reach. Communication is the key to every successful relationship. Intimacy, respect, compassion, and a feeling of connection to others comes from the ability to share thoughts and ideas. Those who want people to listen to them must learn to listen to others themselves. And they must listen without tapping a toe on the ground but with thoughtfulness and patience. Listen with the intent to understand, not reply. Don't raise your voice, improve your argument.

FAITH CHECK

The words we speak have eternal significance. The Bible says that every idle word that men speak, they will have to give account of in the day of judgment (Matthew 12:36). A sobering thought. Give your words meaning without demeaning others. If your heart is with God, speak in love, from your heart. If not, remember that even a fool is considered wise when he keeps his mouth closed.

A fish with its mouth closed never gets caught.

Plumb Tired

Be devoted to one another in brotherly love;
give preference to one another in honor; not lagging
behind in diligence, fervent in spirit, serving the LORD
—ROMANS 12:10–11 NASB

Most of us are so busy all the time, our bodies exist in a state somewhere between tuckered out and running on empty. But being busy isn't always to blame. Living the couch potato life while binge-watching your favorite shows can actually make a person feel more tired than someone who's active. Some people are so lazy they wouldn't bother to chase a snake away! Did you know that laziness and inactivity can be as deadly as smoking and obesity? Our bodies were made to move. People who exercise regularly sleep better, and so do people who give up drinking too much coffee and energy drinks. The ancient Greek physician Hippocrates II, credited as the father of medicine, said, "If we could give every individual the right amount of nourishment and exercise, not too little and not too much, we would have found the safest way to health."

FAITH CHECK

Sometimes it's good to kick back and relax. God knows we all need to rest. He even gave us an entire day, Sunday, as a day to refresh and rest our bodies from the toil of the week. Work diligently at whatever God calls you to do. Rest when you need to. And if you're plastered to a chair or a couch, get moving! "For in Him we live, and move, and have our being" (Acts 17:28 KJV).

I am not an early
bird or a night
owl. Apparently,
I am some sort of
exhausted pigeon.

Enemy Arsenal

Many are the afflictions of the righteous.
—PSALM 34:19 NKJV

There are times in our lives when the enemy throws everything at us, and we suffer a barrage of mishaps and misfortunes, designed to render us helpless, miserable, and low on faith. Satan is envious of God's love and favor on you and your life. A believer who has truly turned over their life to Christ will face storms and trials at some point, and not just once either. Though spiritual warfare takes no vacations, thankfully there are some blessed times of rest and calm in between. These are the times to build up the arsenal of prayer in your life before the next attack. Don't believe the lies of the enemy. When your heart is anguished about your situation and you've cried out to God again and again but you feel like He's not listening, it's understandable to wonder if you've done something to grieve the Lord. But the opposite is true!

FAITH CHECK

This excerpt from a poem by Amy Carmichael says it well: "Pierced are the feet that follow Me...can he have followed far, who has no wound nor scar?" How can a believer truly live by faith if that faith is never tested? Your example of prayerfulness, patient endurance, faithfulness, and hope is an inspiration to others. The devil knows that many others will come to Christ when they see you come through your storm or trial stronger than ever in the Lord.

Satan loads his cannons with big watermelons.

Bringing Out the Best in People

*When I entered your home, you didn't bother to offer me
water to wash the dust from my feet, but she has washed
them with her tears and wiped them with her hair.*

— LUKE 7:44 TLB

Are you the kind of person who encourages, inspires,
and brings out the best in people? Most of us
would like to believe we do but would be hesitant to
answer the question, with good reason. The question
is better answered by those who know you. There are
some people who choose to believe the best of others,
even a serial killer. Though presented with undisputed
facts in criminal court about the individual, they
will doggedly stick to their opinion about the person
they believe in. But God doesn't want or expect us to
wear blinders and pretend everyone we know or meet
is hunky-dory. Instead, He instructs us to be wise as
serpents and gentle as doves (Matthew 10:16). Wise yet
gentle, savvy yet sweet.

FAITH CHECK

The artist Michelangelo believed that every block
of stone has a statue inside of it, and it's the task of
the sculptor to discover it. Jesus didn't take people
at face value either. He saw the possibilities in them.
Where others saw a rag-tag group of fishermen, Jesus
saw faithful disciples. While others disdained to
acknowledge a lowly prostitute, Jesus saw a wounded
woman who would be transformed into a radiant
woman of God.

You see horns.
I see halos.

The Big Letdown

Humble yourselves, therefore, under the mighty hand of God so that at the proper time he may exalt you, casting all your anxieties on him, because he cares for you.

— I PETER 5:6-7 ESV

Disappointment is what you get when you were expecting something else. We are all acquainted with it and it's probably safe to say that none of us like it. However, we can use disappointment to help us grow and succeed. How do you react when things don't turn out the way you hoped they would? Do you keep trying to find another way to achieve your goal, or change your expectations? We tend to see disappointment as either our own personal failure or a real or perceived failure from another person. Sometimes we even feel like God has disappointed us. Has a parent or spouse or friend or pastor ever disappointed you? Dashed your hopes or expectations? If asked the same question, would they say the same thing about you?

FAITH CHECK

Failure gives us the opportunity to learn from an experience, and then move forward toward a different experience, perhaps a successful one. When someone fails us, we also have the opportunity to forgive them and move forward. There are times in each of our lives when we will suffer disappointment, and we will likewise fill the role of the person who does the disappointing.

When life isn't
a bed of roses,
remember Who
wore the thorns.

Dusty Beginnings

*In the same way husbands should love
their wives as their own bodies.*
—EPHESIANS 5:28 ESV

Adam, the first man, was formed by God from the dust of the earth. As a potter forms a vessel out of clay, God created him and breathed life into him. Adam's helpmate, Eve, was not made from dirt but from Adam's rib. Why would God create woman from Adam's body instead of from the earth as well? The answer is in Adam's reaction. Adam immediately recognized Eve as "bone of my bones and flesh of my flesh" (Genesis 2:23 ESV). Our all-wise God knew that no man would ever hate his own flesh. "For no one ever hated his own flesh, but nourishes and cherishes it, just as Christ does the church" (Ephesians 5:29 ESV). God wanted Adam and Eve to love one another, a foreshadowing of Christ's love for the church, His bride.

FAITH CHECK

Adam suffered a wound in his side in order for God to take his rib to create Eve. And Christ, our Savior, suffered a wound in His side from the point of a Roman soldier's spear. Adam's bride came from the wound in his side, and the bride of Christ comes forth from Jesus's blood that was shed for our sins. Genesis 2:24 says that when a man leaves his father and mother and marries, he and his wife become one flesh. And similarly, those who receive Jesus are one with Christ forevermore (Galatians 3:28).

We love because
He first loved us.

—I JOHN 4:19 NIV

Mathematically Speaking

All Scripture is God-breathed and is useful for teaching,
rebuking, correcting and training in righteousness.
—II TIMOTHY 3:16 NIV

It's a fact that four out of three people struggle with math. But not Ivan Panin, a Russian immigrant to the United States. Credited with discovering numeric patterns in the text of both the Hebrew and Greek Bibles, he graduated from Harvard University in 1882, with a master of literary criticism degree. Panin converted to Christianity from agnosticism in 1890, after studying the first chapter of John. He was intrigued by the use of "the" before "God" in one instance, and not in the next: "and the Word was with the God, and the Word was God." To his surprise, he discovered a complex system of mathematical relationships underlying the texts. From that point on until his death in 1942, he meticulously studied these patterns in the Hebrew and Greek texts of the Old and New Testaments, concluding that the patterns could not have been intentionally composed since each author would have to have been a superior mathematician and none were, save for God Himself.

FAITH CHECK

Both the Hebrew and Greek alphabets assign numerical values to letters. Each word, therefore, has a specific numerical value. Panin discovered an incredible, precise structure of vocabulary and the numerical values of words throughout the text of the Bible. But most importantly, this startling discovery led an agnostic to believe in and value God above all else.

I stopped understanding math when the alphabet decided to get involved.

Peach Cobbler

INGREDIENTS:

- 4 cups peeled, sliced peaches (*not canned*)
- 1 cup white sugar
- 1 cup brown sugar
- ½ cup water
- 8 tablespoons butter
- 1½ cups self-rising flour
- 1½ cups milk
- ⅛ teaspoon ground nutmeg
- Ground cinnamon

DIRECTIONS:

1. Preheat oven to 350 degrees.

2. Combine the peaches, one cup brown sugar and water in a saucepan and stir together. Bring to a boil and simmer for ten minutes. Remove from heat.

3. Place the butter in a 3-quart baking dish and put in the oven to melt.

4. Mix remaining one cup of sugar, flour and milk slowly. Do not allow to clump. Pour mixture into the baking dish, directly over the melted butter. Do not stir.

5. Spoon fruit on top, gently pouring in syrup. Sprinkle with ground cinnamon. Bake 30–45 minutes. Batter will rise to top during baking.

6. Serve in a bowl over a scoop of vanilla bean ice cream.

If I were
any peachier,
I'd be a
cobbler!

Our Chapter

In the former account [which I prepared], O Theophilus,
I made a [continuous report] dealing with all the
things which Jesus began to do and to teach.

—ACTS 1:1 AMP

The apostles in the Gospel of Luke were very different from the brave and courageous men we read about in the Book of Acts. When they witnessed Jesus nailed to the cross, they thought their dreams and hopes in Him as the Messiah died with Him. That is, until the third day! When Jesus rose from the dead and revealed Himself to His followers, their faith and hope rose with Him. They truly understood Jesus as the Resurrection and the Life, connecting the Old Testament dots to the New Testament gospel written on their hearts. No longer fearful, or in hiding, or full of doubt, they began to preach the truth with boldness and confidence.

A new life in Christ can sometimes begin with such doubts and fears. We worry about what family and friends will think of us, that we will be rejected or ridiculed. However, the more a believer studies scripture and seeks God in prayer, the more he or she will know—and grow in Christ. As faith increases, fear decreases.

FAITH CHECK

Although we can read from the beginning to the end of the Book of Acts, we should think of the book as ongoing and unfinished. Believers will continue to add to this heavenly accounting daily, with their faithful prayers and acts, obedience in their walk, and sacrifice, until the day that Jesus returns triumphantly to the earth.

Every faithful believer will eventually attain a Ph.D in the gospel: Past-having-Doubt.

Who You Are

But ye [are] a chosen generation, a royal priesthood,
a holy nation, a peculiar people; that ye should
shew forth the praises of Him who hath called you
out of darkness into His marvellous light.
—I PETER 2:9 KJV

One of Nancy Drew's dearest friends in the fictional town of River Heights was Bess, a character you couldn't help but feel sorry for. In every book in the earlier versions of the popular series, she was described as "plump Bess," or a "pretty, slightly plump blonde." It's human nature to label other people by the way they look, their mannerisms, status, or ethnicity, but overall without malice. If someone is smart, their nickname might be Brains, or Harvard. A rich person might be called Booshi, which is a misspelled derivative of the word *bourgeoisie*, meaning "people of aristocratic privilege." Skinny people are called String Beans, individuals who wear glasses are Four-eyes, and environmentally conscious folk are called Tree-huggers. The extreme end of the labeling spectrum ends in racism and hatred, a place no lover of Christ should ever be found.

FAITH CHECK

The nicknames or designations other people tag us with can be aggravating, but the real issue is what we think of ourselves. Sometimes we start to believe what others say about us. Jesus asked His disciples, "Who do you say that I am?" After a couple of wrong answers from the other disciples, Peter declared, "You are the Messiah" (Mark 8:29 NIV). Who does Jesus Christ say that *you* are?

I hate it when I see some old person and then realize we went to school together.

The Fiery Serpents

So the LORD sent poisonous snakes among them to
punish them, and many of them were bitten and died.
— NUMBERS 21:6 TLB

The Israelites were tired of their seemingly aimless wanderings and began murmuring and complaining about Moses and the "light bread," the daily manna God provided. Well, God had had enough of their crybaby attitude! He sent fiery serpents among them, so-called because of either their reddish hue or their venom that burned like fire through flesh. But the people began to cry out, asking God's forgiveness, and Moses prayed for the people. God relented and told Moses to make a brass image of the fiery serpent. The serpent is a creature cursed above all others (Genesis 3:14), but in this case, the image became a symbol of death and healing. When the brass serpent was lifted up, any person dying from a snake bite who looked to that symbol would be miraculously healed.

FAITH CHECK

We are all born into sin, yet we have a daily choice to either continue in our sins or ask God to forgive us. When that old serpent, Satan, sinks his fangs into us, injecting us with the deadly temptation of sin, our miraculous cure is to look up to Jesus, who was nailed to a wooden cross, a symbol of death, and lifted up for all to behold. He became sin for us and gave His life that we might live eternally with Him. Look up to Jesus, who endured the cross that we might live.

My sin was great,
but Your love
was greater.

Job's Wife

God said to Satan, "Have you noticed my friend Job?
There is no one quite like him—honest and true to
his word, totally devoted to God and hating evil."
—JOB 1:8 THE MESSAGE

Job's wife was a princess, married to a tribal leader, the richest and most influential of all the men in the east, but also a faithful man beloved of God. She is mostly known for giving her husband some uplifting advice, "Curse God and die" (Job 2:9), when he was in the midst of his pain and torment. That phrase has echoed through the centuries as an example of what *not* to say to someone going through a trial. But consider this: Job's wife suffered some of the same afflictions he suffered—the loss of their ten children, seven sons and three daughters, and of everything they owned. However, there is no mention of her grief. "Your children were having a party at the home of the oldest brother when a tornado swept in off the desert and struck the house. It collapsed on the young people and they died..." (Job 1:18–19 THE MESSAGE). Instead of turning to God in her mourning, she seemed to have turned away, thus becoming a mouthpiece for Satan against her husband. Her faith broke along with her heart, and neither was ever healed.

FAITH CHECK

Sometime during her husband's affliction, Job's wife disappears from the account and is no longer mentioned. At the end of Job's afflictions, God doubled His servant's fortune, and Job married a young woman who bore him ten children—seven sons and three daughters.

So often we think that to be encouragers we have to produce great words of wisdom when, in fact, a few simple syllables of sympathy and an arm around the shoulder can often provide much-needed comfort.

—FLORENCE LITTAUER

The Mail Will Not Fail

Therefore, we are ambassadors for Christ,
God making His appeal through us.
—II CORINTHIANS 5:20 ESV

Do you recall the motto of the United States Postal Service? It goes like this: "Neither snow nor rain nor heat nor gloom of night stays these couriers from the swift completion of their appointed rounds." The words originated from an ancient writing, *The Persian Wars,* by the Greek historian Herodotus and are chiseled in stone over the entrance of the New York City Postal Service on Eighth Avenue. The Postal Service lays no claim to an "official" motto, yet the noble words seem to fit the job description.

Each believer is a carrier of God's Word, and the message of Good News. In Mark 16:15 NIV, Christ tells us to "go into all the world and preach the gospel to all creation." If believers were to have a motto for their God-appointed task as ambassadors to the world, this would be it.

FAITH CHECK

Whenever we mail a package, a post office clerk always asks the same question, "Does your package contain anything fragile, liquid, perishable, or potentially hazardous?" The message of the gospel is precious, not fragile. There is liquid, in redemption through the blood of Christ. Our lives are perishable, but we are promised eternal life through Jesus. And God's Word is indeed hazardous, but only to sin.

It is a
well-known fact
that bills travel
through the mail
at twice the
speed of checks.

Follow That Star

And she gave birth to her firstborn son and wrapped him in swaddling clothes and laid him in a manger, because there was no place for them in the inn.

—LUKE 2:6 ESV

Shepherds were not what you call "fancy" folks back in those days. In those days people turned up their noses up at them because shepherds were unable to keep the ceremonial laws and rules due to their trade. They were seen as uneducated, smelly, and undignified. Yet God chose to send His angels to these men rather than to the learned men of the temple. It was traditional in those days to have local musicians come to the house after the birth of a male child, in order to greet his entrance into the world with music. Since there would be no such rejoicing in the stable where Jesus was born, God sent His angels instead to sing songs from heaven, to rejoice, and to herald the birth of His Son in the skies above. "...Everything must be fulfilled that is written about me in the law of Moses, the Prophets and the Psalms" (Luke 24:24 NIV).

FAITH CHECK

After traveling eighty miles from Nazareth to Bethlehem for the census, Mary and Joseph could find no lodgings and had to settle for a stable. Imagine how frightened and lonely Mary must have felt as a young woman giving birth without the support of her mother, or even a midwife. On that glorious night, there was no room at the inn for Jesus to be born. On this earth, there was only room for Him on a rough-hewn cross at Golgotha. Is there room in *your* heart for Him today?

O little town of Bethlehem, how still we see thee lie! Above thy deep and dreamless sleep, the silent stars go by.

—PHILLIPS BROOKS

You Are My Sunshine

The race is not to the swift.
—ECCLESIASTES 9:11 NIV

The song "You Are My Sunshine," was a popular tune written in 1939. It gained wide recognition with Jimmie H. Davis, a country music singer as well as governor of Louisiana in the years 1944–1948 and 1960–1964. Born in a two-room shack to sharecropper parents, he was one of eleven children who worked long days in the cotton fields. He discovered early on that he could pick out chords on a guitar and sing even though he couldn't read or write music. His music career took off, but he later decided to pursue public office and used his songs as a means of connecting with voters. During his first campaign, he would often sing one of his many songs instead of answering politically contentious questions. Davis seemed to understand early on the theater aspect of politics and populism, so much so that after his election he was known as "The Singing Governor." One of his solid accomplishments in his two terms as governor was establishing a state driver's license certification. Before this legislation, all anyone had to do to drive a car in Louisiana was to turn on the ignition and hit the gas pedal.

FAITH CHECK

We cannot predict those who will rise to fame and fortune, to power, to thrones, or to public office. God looks at heart qualifications, not at degrees or honor or experience. Man elects, but God selects, according to His plan and purpose. "The race is not to the swift, or the battle to the strong...but time and chance happen to them all" (Ecclesiastes 9:11 NIV).

Just living is not enough...one must have sunshine, freedom, and a little flower.

—HANS CHRISTIAN ANDERSON

Beyond the Pale

The LORD will sustain him upon his sickbed,
in his illness, You restore him to health.
—PSALM 41:3 NASB

Waiting for the results of a crucial medical test is an excruciating ordeal. Sometimes the outcome is good and one can breathe a sigh of relief. But when the results are not good, and the doctor says those words your ears don't want to hear, your entire life comes crashing down around you. Time is divided from this point on: before the results and after the results. Personal goals, heart motives, the way we look at people and situations all change. Suddenly, the weight of all the opportunities, special moments, and wasted years crushes the spirit. The road behind you seems so long, yet the journey ahead is cut short too quickly. A bad prognosis sounds like a death sentence. Some people, including medical professionals, are ever-hopeful optimists, who truly believe that God can do anything. Others will hear of your prognosis and begin to carve your tombstone in their minds, as if you are already gone to them.

FAITH CHECK

The truth is, your life isn't over until God says it's over. As nineteenth-century pastor and Christian evangelist George Mueller once said, "Faith does not operate in the realm of the possible.... Faith begins where man's power ends." You might be a miracle waiting to happen. Trust God as your Alpha and Omega. He is the God of our beginning and our end.

Don't believe in miracles—depend on them.

—LAURENCE J. PETER

Monumental Mistakes

If we say that we have no sin, we are deceiving
ourselves and the truth is not in us.
—I JOHN 1:8 NASB

Everyone makes mistakes, but some failures are bigger than others. When presenters Warren Beatty and Faye Dunaway announced the wrong Best Picture winner at the 2017 Academy Awards, the Oscar went to "embarrassment." Designers of the *Titanic* considered the ship to be unsinkable, and under-equipped the vessel with lifeboats—a disastrous decision. Believe it or not, NASA accidentally taped over the original footage of the historic 1969 moon landing! The tapes were inadvertently included in a batch of 200,000 other tapes that were magnetically erased and reused to save money. A publishing company made a whopper of a mistake in 1631, printing a Bible with a terrible typo in the Ten Commandments passage: "Thou shalt commit adultery." Now referred to as the "Sinners' Bible" and the "Adulterers Bible," only nine known copies of this infamous version exist today. The release of the Bible caused both uproar and outrage in England. King Charles I was furious, ordering the Bibles to be destroyed.

FAITH CHECK

We all make mistakes, but leaving the "not" out when it comes to sin is the biggest mistake any of us could ever make.

When we learn from experience, the scars of sin can lead us to restoration and a renewed intimacy with God.

—CHARLES STANLEY

The Last Chance Cafe

*And he causeth all, both small and great, rich
and poor, free and bond, to receive a mark in
their right hand, or in their foreheads.*
—REVELATION 13:16 KJV

Esau came back home tired and hungry from hunting all day and got a waft of some of his brother Jacob's savory red lentil stew on the open fire. In addition to being a mama's boy, Jacob was a good cook. Seeing a shrewd opportunity, Jacob took advantage of his brother, suggesting a trade: his birthright for a bowl (Genesis 25:29–34). Now remember, Esau was not starving. But he readily agreed to sell his birthright for some stew and a piece of bread to satisfy his belly. Esau cared so little about his birthright because he believed he could make his own destiny. After all, he was a hunter who chased down what he wanted in life. Jacob went about things differently. Instead of trusting God for his destiny, Jacob relied on deceit and trickery to get what he wanted. Both had regrets. The difference between the two is that Jacob ultimately submitted to God, and God transformed him, even giving him a new name, Israel, to reflect his new character (Genesis 32:28).

FAITH CHECK

At the end of the age, mankind will be given a choice—to take the mark of the beast or die. The enemy will entice many to take the mark because of the "benefits" he will offer. Food and water in a world of famine, order in chaos and violence, and many other empty promises. Many, like Esau, will choose their belly over their birthright. Others will treasure their birthright in Christ, no matter the consequence.

Esau was a hairy man, hairy back and hairy hands.

—THE DUNAWAYS

Cuss Words

From the same mouth come blessing and cursing. Does a spring pour forth from the same opening both fresh and salt water?
—JAMES 3:10-11 ESV

Have you ever been stuck in the vicinity of someone who uses curse words like commas? It's a miserable position for a believer to be in. Anywhere and everywhere, we seem to encounter people who have no problem spewing out expletives. The way of the world is way different from the way Christ-followers live their lives. Words that are no more than "sentence enhancers" for some folks grate like sandpaper against others. And those who mix up the Lord's name in their crude and lewd epithets are especially hard to tolerate. Those who know you should be well aware that *you* don't curse. Cursing is the enemy's vocabulary, not the language of God. No matter the excuse or provocation, cursing has no part in a life that is right with Christ.

FAITH CHECK

Be honest with those you are closest to. Tell them that curse words bother you and make you feel uncomfortable. And if you use cuss words, repent and ask forgiveness. "But now you must put them all away: anger, wrath, malice, slander, and obscene talk from your mouth" (Colossians 3:8 ESV). Pray for the pro-profanity people in your life, and sweeten your own words by reading God's Word daily.

He cussed from
A to Z, but he
kept stopping at
certain letters.

Strawberry Muffins

INGREDIENTS:

- 1⅔ cups fresh strawberries, finely diced
- ⅔ cup sugar
- ⅓ cup melted butter
- 2 eggs
- 1½ cups all-purpose flour
- ½ teaspoon baking soda
- ½ teaspoon salt
- ½ teaspoon cinnamon

DIRECTIONS:

1. Heat oven to 425 degrees. Line a regular 12-cup muffin tin with paper baking cups.

2. Lightly smash the strawberries in a bowl with a fork.

3. Stir in sugar, butter and eggs.

4. Add remaining ingredients and stir till moistened.

5. Spoon batter into baking cups.

6. Bake 15-18 minutes until light golden brown, or until toothpick poked into center comes out clean.

7. Cool five minutes. Remove muffins from pan. Enjoy! Serves 12.

The strawberry grows underneath the nettle. And wholesome berries thrive and ripen best neighbour'd by fruit of baser quality.

—WILLIAM SHAKESPEARE

Fuel for Thought

For since the creation of the world His invisible
attributes are clearly seen, being understood by
the things that are made, even His eternal power
and Godhead, so that they are without excuse.
—ROMANS 1:20 NKJV

While working deep underneath the ground, coal miners are known to marvel at the surprising natural artwork revealed by mechanical disturbance, the imprint of ancient plants, insects, shells, and bones on the walls they scrape away at each day. And why wouldn't they see such sights? Coal deposits are basically petrified peat swamps. Peat is a substance made from decaying plants before they transform into rock. Feathery fronds, large leaves, gigantic ferns, and trees that look like giant asparagus spears decorate the walls like an artist's canvas. Such sights remind us of hidden history buried under the earth by time and circumstance.

FAITH CHECK

God has left His thumbprint on all of His creation, yet those who live and work in the light of day often miss the beauty of His labor. Let us not take for granted the breathtaking vistas of mountains and seas and great billowing clouds that cast shadows across fields of wheat, the stars and constellations twinkling above, the intricacies of a snowflake, and the miracle and perfection of the human body, made in God's own image. "For I am fearfully and wonderfully made: marvellous are thy works; and that my soul knoweth right well" (Psalm 139:14 KJV).

The most
important thing
to come out of
a mine is
the miner.

Rubs You the Wrong Way

For the LORD sees not as man sees: man looks on the
outward appearance, but the LORD looks on the heart.
—I SAMUEL 16:7 ESV

If you've ever stroked a cat or dog's coat, you are well
aware of the visual of rubbing their fur the wrong
way. People can rub us the wrong way too. We've all
experienced someone who has had that effect on us.
And we will again. Such is life! The truth is, some folks
are in need of a personality overhaul. Like nonstop
talkers who dominate the conversation at a gathering,
refusing to listen to anyone else. Or a dinner guest who
piles their plate high with mashed potatoes and passes
a near-empty plate along. How about someone who
says mean things about you or your family behind your
back? Or a neighbor who borrows your lawn mower or
other items and never returns them? Folks like this
can be annoying and downright aggravating. But what
we see and what God sees are as different as can be.
That abrasive or obnoxious person might be a lump of
coal that will one day be transformed into a diamond.
You might have been a diamond-in-the-rough as well
but God's Word transformed you, and He can transform
them too.

FAITH CHECK
All of humanity begins life under the curse of sin, no
matter our birth, status, education, or knowledge of
social graces. We are rough, stained, torn, and ugly, yet
we are all invited to dine in honor at the Master's table.
Come as you are to God, and He will transform you into
a new creature, an eternal son, an eternal daughter.
Loved and accepted. Sparkling and new.

He's been through the mill, but he ain't refined.

—ROSE COSTANZA

The Power of the Open Grave

And many bodies of the saints who had fallen asleep were
raised; and coming out of the tombs after his resurrection,
they went into the holy city and appeared to many.
—MATTHEW 27:52-53 NKJV

At the very moment Jesus exhaled His final breath
on the cross, a great earthquake shook the land,
the temple veil was torn in two from top to bottom, and
the graves of the righteous were opened. Most graves
in the area were hewn from solid rocks, carved out of
crevices, or were natural caves. The earthquake opened
these sepulchers to the light of day and they lay open
for the duration of the Passover, since it was unlawful
to bury anyone during that time. Much to the distress
of loved ones and officials, the bodies lay exposed to the
elements. However, on the third day, the day of Jesus's
resurrection, the dead rose from their tombs and began
to walk, just as Lazarus had when Jesus summoned
him from death to life. They walked in the city and
appeared to many, reuniting with loved ones.

FAITH CHECK

God knows the resting place of every one of His
redeemed, whether that individual's physical body lies
in a tomb, at the bottom of the sea, or is reduced to
ashes scattered to the winds. For all who die in Christ
will be resurrected as Jesus Himself was resurrected
as the first fruits of the harvest (I Corinthians 15:23),
from death to life eternal.

Do not be amazed at this, for a time is coming when all who are in their graves will hear his voice.

—JOHN 5:28 NIV

Duck, Duck, Goose

For I know the plans I have for you, declares the LORD, plans
for welfare and not for evil, to give you a future and a hope.
—JEREMIAH 29:11 ESV

Duck, Duck, Goose is a classic playground game most
of us are familiar with. Children sit in a circle. One
person is the "Goose" and walks on the outside of the
circle tapping everyone on the head. Duck. Duck. Duck.
Goose! The kid who is tagged "goose" by the old goose
must get up and chase the other kid around the circle
before the he or she sits in their empty space. If the
old goose succeeds in stealing the spot, the new goose
starts the process over again. Being a duck was safe,
but ordinary and kind of boring. All the ducks ever did
was sit in a circle. But being a goose was everything.
You got to decide who you wanted the new goose to be,
and if that kid happened to be a kid you had a crush
on, you didn't mind being chased around the circle a
few times until you stole their empty spot. A game is a
game after all. No one wants to lose.

FAITH CHECK

Do you ever feel as if people are trying to cubbyhole
who you are in life? "You're a duck." You've always been
a duck and you will never be anything but a duck. You
aren't meant to make tough choices or take chances
or chase after your dreams. Or, "You're a goose." You'll
never settle down or sit still in one place for long. You
are a risk-taker, unstable, and undependable. Time
to cry "fowl!" God says you are His child and you are
exactly who He created you to be.

Be yourself, because
an original is worth
more than a copy.

What's the Skinny?

Surely the LORD God does nothing unless He reveals
His secret counsel to His servants the prophets.
—AMOS 3:7 NASB

Military orders issued by the Marine Corps from World War II until the late 1960s were copied on paper that resembled the translucent skin of an onion. The paper was extremely thin and fragile. So, before long the enlisted men started asking the office personnel, "What's the skinny on promotions?" This question soon became synonymous with inside information, the details, or the confidential scoop. In the Old Testament, God revealed His plans, judgments, and blessings upon His people through His prophets. The prophet Amos gave a somber prophecy concerning the destruction of eight nations. This warning included the Israelites due to their willful and continued disobedience to God in spite of the warnings He had sent through many prophets. God posed His own question in this warning. "Can two walk together, unless they are agreed?" (Amos 3:3 NKJV). Israel was in defiant disagreement with God, having turned to idol worship and all manner of depravity. In spite of this warning, they still chose not to repent.

FAITH CHECK
New Testament Christ-followers can hear from God directly, because He dwells in the hearts of those who believe. God gives us the skinny on how to live our lives through His Word, the Bible, and He never fails to answer our prayers. Those who live a right life of obedience and devotion will never have a problem walking with God.

When you walk
with God each day,
there's no chance
of getting lost.

Jephthah's Vow

If a man makes a vow to the LORD he shall
not violate his word; he shall do according
to all that proceeds out of his mouth.
—NUMBERS 30:2 NASB

Jephthah had a reputation as a fierce warrior, so much so that when Ammon made war on Israel, the men of Gilead sought him and his men to defend them. But Jephthah wanted them to make him their leader, and they agreed. So, "The Spirit of the LORD came upon Jephthah" (Judges 11:29 NASB), and he soon returned from a great victory over the Ammonites. But Jephthah had made a reckless vow: if he was victorious, whatever came out the doors of his house to meet him first, he would offer as a burnt offering to God (Judges 11:30–31 NKJV). However, when he saw who came out first, he tore his clothes and was filled with grief. His only child, his precious daughter, came out dancing with timbrels and rejoicing at her father's victory.

FAITH CHECK

Though such an offering would have been unacceptable to the Lord, Jephthah's daughter accepted her fate, reacting nobly to her father's solemn vow to God. She asked him for two months to be with her friends in order to mourn her virginity. Perhaps instead of dying, she lived as a perpetual servant of the tabernacle, never marrying, never bouncing a child on her knees.

Though his vow cost him everything precious to his heart, Jephthah would not go back on his promise to God. How many of us are as faithful to our promises to God?

When I make
a vow to God, then
I would suggest
to you that's even
stronger than a
handshake in Texas.

—RICK PERRY

Flight of the Monarchs

Therefore, if anyone is in Christ, he is a new creation.
The old has passed away; behold, the new has come.
—II CORINTHIANS 5:17 ESV

Monarch butterflies are beautiful, delicate, stained-glass creations of God that sail through the air. They begin their life cycle as eggs attached to a milkweed plant and hatch as larvae. The larvae consume their eggshells and the plant they hatched on, transforming into plump caterpillars. Eventually the colorful caterpillars create a hard case around their body as they enter the pupa stage, later emerging as black, orange, and white butterflies. Though there are four generations of monarchs, the first three live for only two to six weeks. Only one generation, born in September and October, will be sturdy enough to make the annual migration to warmer climates in Mexico and California and will live for six to eight weeks, an eternity to a butterfly. Like the monarch butterfly, we begin life in a very different state. When we repent of our sins and receive Jesus Christ into our hearts, we are transformed into new creatures. Our metamorphosis is a complete and utter change, from death to life eternal.

FAITH CHECK

Believers go to heaven when their time on earth is done (I Peter 2:9), and they will dwell there with God forever in His marvelous light. Those who trust in the Lord in the here-and-now will live eternally with Him in the hereafter. Though we are born into sin, we do not have to die in sin, for God in His tender mercy has given us a choice.

Butterflies are flowers that fly and all but sing.

—ROBERT FROST.

Happily Ever After

And to present her to himself as a radiant church, without stain or wrinkle or any other blemish, but holy and blameless.
—EPHESIANS 5:26 NIV

In the time of Christ, Jewish weddings consisted of very specific traditions. The first step was the betrothal. The groom would travel from his father's house to the home of his prospective bride. He would pay the "purchase price," in order to establish the marriage covenant, and would then return to his father's house for about twelve months. During that time, he'd prepare a place, a house for the couple to live happily ever after in. After this, the groom would surprise his bride at a time of his father's choosing, unknown to her, and hold a small private marriage ceremony. The final step of the marriage ceremony was for the groom to return to his father's house with his bride to consummate the marriage and celebrate their wedding for the next seven days with family and friends and a multitude of guests.

FAITH CHECK

Jesus came to earth from His Father's house to be betrothed to His bride, the church. He gave His life for us on the cross, before rising from death to life and returning to His father's house to prepare a place for us. And when Jesus returns from heaven to earth for His bride, there will be a great wedding feast, the celebration of all celebrations (Revelation 19:6-9 ESV). The truest happily-ever-after story that will ever be!

For the Christian,
Heaven is where
Jesus is. We do not
need to speculate on
what heaven will be
like. It is enough to
know that we will be
forever with Him.

—WILLIAM BARCLAY

Mustard Seeds

For if you had faith even as small as a tiny mustard
seed, you could say to this mountain, 'Move!' and it
would go far away. Nothing would be impossible.
—MATTHEW 17:20 TLB

Grind up a cup of mustard seeds, add some vinegar,
and *voilà*, you have a tangy yellow condiment most
often squeezed onto grilled hot dogs or added to potato
salad. Mustard seeds are tiny, round seeds measuring
about 0.05 of an inch and are similar in size to a sesame
seed. But don't be fooled by their size. There's an old
saying that big things often have small beginnings,
which is especially true of the mustard seed. The
mature plants can grow to a height of between six and
twenty feet with a twenty-foot spread, or even taller
under the right circumstances. And under the right
conditions, faith can grow that way too.

FAITH CHECK

You cannot pick an apple from an apple seed, but one
apple seed can potentially grow a tree that produces
many apples. "Mustard seed faith" is a small beginning
indeed. Within that vital seed of faith is the potential
for a believer's confidence in God to grow. Our personal
testimony begins when we are rooted in Christ through
salvation, and our faith grows through our experience
with God as we learn to trust Him. Faith can flourish
and grow to towering heights, just as a mustard seed
grows into an enormous plant. The law of "root and
fruit" is to grow roots downward and bear fruit upward
(Isaiah 37:31–32). A seed of faith is a mighty beginning!

So never lose an opportunity of urging a practical beginning, however small, for it is wonderful how often in such matters the mustard seed germinates and roots itself.

—FLORENCE NIGHTINGALE

Eclipse

The sun shall be turned into darkness and the moon into
blood, before the great and terrible day of the LORD come.
—JOEL 2:31 KJV

During a total eclipse, the entire sun is covered
for a few minutes by the moon as it moves in
front of the sun. For those few minutes, the earth is
darkened. Animals and insects react as if night has
fallen. Songbirds go silent, chickens begin to roost,
and mosquitoes start biting. Tides change too, and
so do shadows. The shadows of leaves exhibit curious
crescent shapes on the ground.

Jesus warned that immediately after the tribulation
(Matthew 24:29–30), the sun would be darkened and
the moon would not give its light, the stars would
fall from heaven and the powers of heaven would be
shaken before His return. Every person on earth, from
every tribe, nation, and tongue, will see the Son of Man
returning to earth on the clouds of heaven with power
and great glory.

FAITH CHECK

Think of an eclipse as more than just a natural wonder.
Perhaps an eclipse is a reminder to us of Who is in
charge. The warmth of sunlight, the air we breathe,
the food we eat are all elements of our life that we take
for granted. On that great and terrible day of the Lord,
when Jesus returns, many will recognize and realize
too late who He truly is. And a fatal darkness will fall
for them, a permanent eclipse. Those who reject Christ
will never again see the Light or feel the warmth of His
love. The darkness they once embraced will be their
portion forever.

When we have God in clear focus, His powerful presence eclipses our fear.

—CHARLES R. SWINDOLL

Perfect Southern Sweet Tea

Iced tea is the perfect thirst-quencher on a hot day, and Southerners enjoy the beverage so much they like to brag that they're raised on sweet tea and Jesus. Some folks drink bottled or canned tea, but southern tradition dictates that one must drink authentic homemade tea brewed strong, cold and sweet.

INGREDIENTS:

- 6–8 Family-sized tea bags
- 6 cups (one quart) boiling water.
- 12 cups (three quarts) cool water
- 1½ cups sugar (or to taste)
- ¼ teaspoon baking soda

DIRECTIONS:

1. Sprinkle baking soda into a large stockpot. Add the tea bags to the pot. Pour the 6 cups of boiling water over the tea bags. Cover the pot and allow the mixture to steep for at least 15 minutes.

2. Carefully remove the tea bags with a slotted spoon. Then pour the steeped tea into a pitcher. Add sugar and stir until the sugar is completely dissolved. Add cool water. Refrigerate until tea is chilled.

3. Pour tea into glasses filled with ice. Garnish with a slice of lemon, a sprig of mint or a small slice of watermelon.

Iced tea is too pure and natural a creation not to have been invented as soon as tea, ice, and hot weather crossed paths.

—JOHN EGERTON

A Cana Catastrophe

There was a wedding in Cana of Galilee, and the mother of Jesus was there.... And when they ran out of wine, the mother of Jesus said to Him: "They have no wine."

—JOHN 2:1-2 NKJV

Cana was a little town about a stone's throw from Nazareth. Because of its location and the guest list—Mary, Jesus, and His disciples—the marriage celebration was likely that of a family of modest circumstance. Rich people would never have invited peasants to a wedding celebration. Even if a family was dirt poor, weddings were quite a big to-do in Jewish culture. These were no three-hour celebrations with a deejay and a buffet. The groom's family would be responsible for providing all the refreshments for the *week-long* festivities. At this particular wedding, the unthinkable happened. The hosts discovered they were running out of wine, and that was a social disgrace. Maybe the family didn't have the money to buy more. Whatever the reason, Mary went straight to her son Jesus and asked Him for help. What kind of help? Did Mary know something about her son that no one else knew?

FAITH CHECK

Is it difficult to imagine that Jesus might have helped His mother miraculously a few times in the years prior to beginning His ministry? At any rate, Mary told the servants to do whatever her son told them to do, and Jesus turned the water into wine. When we bring our problems and our needs to Christ, we are putting our faith in the One who makes all things possible.

To turn water into wine, and what is common into what is holy, is indeed the glory of Christianity.

—FREDERICK WILLIAM ROBERTSON

Baby Names

And I went unto the prophetess; and she
conceived, and bare a son. Then said the LORD
to me, Call his name Mahershalalhashbaz.
—ISAIAH 8:3 KJV

One of the longest names in the Bible is Mahershalalhashbaz, the name of the prophet Isaiah's second son. Try tackling that word in a spelling bee or even pronouncing it. Mahershalalhashbaz means, "Hurry to the spoils!" or "He has made haste to the plunder!" God gave Isaiah the baby's name as a symbol of the destruction of Damascus and Samaria by the Assyrians that would come very early in the child's life. Another God-assigned name is Methuselah, which means, "His death shall bring judgment," or "When he is dead it shall be sent" (Genesis 5). This, of course, referred to the great flood, which came in the year that Methuselah died. God also gave the prophet Hosea names for his children that were prophetic messages about judgments on Israel. God gives a new name to His people, reflecting a heart change and transformation in character.

FAITH CHECK

God changed Abram's name to Abraham, which means "father of a multitude." Jacob's name meant "supplanter," and God changed his name to Israel after an intense wrestling match. Jesus gave James and John the nickname Boanerges, meaning "sons of thunder" (Mark 3:17). Best of all, God will give a new name to all who overcome in the end (Revelation 2:17).

A good character is
the best tombstone.
Those who loved you
and were helped by you
will remember you when
forget-me-nots have
withered. Carve your name
on hearts, not on marble.

—CHARLES SPURGEON

This Is Our Father's House

Do not be conformed to this world, but be transformed by the renewal of your mind, that by testing you may discern what is the will of God, what is good and acceptable and perfect.
—ROMANS 12:02 ESV

A few generations ago, there were no ifs, ands, or buts about it—you washed behind your ears and put on your Sunday-best clothes to wear to church. It didn't matter if you were rich or poor, you pressed the best of whatever you had hanging in your closet, spit-shined your shoes, and entered the service with a smile on your face. In Victorian times people of means made a point of distinguishing themselves from the lower socioeconomic classes. But with the rise of the middle class and manufactured clothing, everyone began to step up their church fashion. In the eighteenth and nineteenth centuries, certain ministers and Christian groups began to speak out against the practice of parading finery in the pews. Charles Finney and other preachers praised plain, simple clothing. John Wesley viewed fashion and faith as sinful, preaching instead a gospel of plainness. For a time, fancy was out, and frumpy was in. Not for long, though.

FAITH CHECK

Nowadays, most people wear whatever they fancy in place of fancy clothes. Perhaps there is a middle ground. Why not embrace modesty and decency in the choice of our church apparel instead of over or under dressing (I Timothy 2:9)? For those who are clothed in God's righteousness, what we wear to church isn't as important as our heart attitude.

Life ain't
no dress
rehearsal.

Braille

The LORD opens the eyes of the blind.
—PSALM 146:8 ESV

The tiny raised dots can be found almost everywhere if you look for them. Braille is on drive-thru ATMs, elevator control panels, and all public transportation. A little boy in France named Louis Braille was playing in his father's shop when he injured one of his eyes. Even though he received treatment for the injury, it became infected and doctors were unable to prevent the infection from spreading to the other eye. Little Louis became totally blind at the tender age of three. Later, he enrolled in the National Institute for the Blind in Paris. Louis's teacher invited a man who had developed a "night-writing" system for the military to come and speak to the students. The system used raised dots but was far too complex. However, Louis was inspired and in 1825 began to experiment, soon developing his own code of six dots arranged in two parallel rows. Each set of rows represented a letter of the alphabet. The new system was simple and easy for students to learn. Braille soon became popular with the other students, but Louis Braille's system, even at his own school, was not widely accepted for many years.

FAITH CHECK

A tragic accident changed a child's life forever, but as a young man, Louis Braille opened a whole new world of communication, reading, and knowledge for those without sight. And what is even more wonderful is that even though there are many books available in braille, the Bible has been transcribed into forty languages for those who are blind and want to see—with their heart.

Braille is knowledge, and knowledge is power.

—LOUIS BRAILLE

SOS

God is our refuge and strength, a very present help in trouble.
—PSALM 46:1 NKJV

Most people have heard of the universal distress signal known as an SOS, but if you ask what the letters stand for, not many will be able to give the right answer. Some people believe that SOS stands for "Save Our Ship," or "Save Our Souls," but neither answer is correct. The continuous Morse code signal with no spaces or stops is a string of three dots, three dashes, followed by three dots (...---...). Three dots in Morse code form the letter *S*, and three dashes are an *O*, so people started calling the distress signal an SOS. Since then, countless people have called out for help all over the world using this universal distress signal, and someone somewhere has come to their rescue.

FAITH CHECK

How do you call out to God for help when you're in trouble? Whether you fall prostrate on the ground or on your knees and call out, "Help me, Jesus!" in a loud voice, or simply ask for help with the barest wisp of a breath, or even cry out silently with an anguished heart, God will answer you and come to your rescue. "Call upon Me in the day of trouble; I shall rescue you, and you will honor Me" (Psalm 50:15 NASB).

In old western movies, settlers would cry out, "Here comes the cavalry!" when they were about to be rescued. But our greatest Hero, Jesus Christ, gave His life for all of mankind at Calvary and rescued us forever.

Smooth Sailing

I have said these things to you, that in me you may
have peace. In the world you will have tribulation.
But take heart; I have overcome the world.
—JOHN 16:33 ESV

There are two important birthdays in a believer's
life: the day they are born and the day they are
born again. Some believers are under the mistaken
assumption that everything will be strawberries and
cream from the moment they say yes to Christ. But
that way of thinking is faulty. There will be trials,
tribulations, and troubles in life. Jesus said so! (John
16:33). If everything was perfect and easy, we'd never
have to utilize our faith to overcome. Smooth waters
do not make skillful sailors. His Word, the Bible, is
our most effective weapon of warfare to defeat the
enemy, but we must know how to speak His Word over
the storms of life. "Yet in all these things we are more
than conquerors through Him who loved us" (Romans
8:37 NKJV). The Bible is also our means of navigation
through the journey of life. If you are facing in the right
direction, all you need to do is stay on course, right?
Sounds easy. But staying on course is more difficult
than it seems.

FAITH CHECK

The Roman philosopher Seneca said, "If one does not
know to which port one is sailing, no wind is favorable."
Which port are you sailing to? If you're not headed in
the right direction, it's not too late to change course.

God never said the journey would be easy, but He did say that the arrival would be worthwhile.

—MAX LUCADO

Hemmed in Prayer

And there was a woman who had had a discharge of blood
for twelve years, and though she had spent all her living
on physicians, she could not be healed by anyone.

—LUKE 8:43 ESV

Surrounded by a dense crowd of people, all clamoring for His attention, Jesus suddenly asked, "Who touched Me?" His disciples threw up their hands. How could Jesus expect to know who touched Him in the midst of wall-to-wall people? But His eyes were on a trembling woman who fell down before Jesus and confessed. Ceremonially unclean by a "monthly" flow of blood that continued for twelve years, her admission was embarrassing and shameful. Banned from all human contact, the woman was a lonely outcast, a social leper. She'd spent everything she had on doctors and remained sick, weak, and miserable. The woman with the issue of blood had nothing left. Desperate, she touched the fringe called the *tzitzit* on the hem of Jesus's prayer shawl, a *"tallit."* On the four corners are fringe with special knots or tassels, interwoven with a blue thread used by the faithful to remember and count the commandments (Numbers 15:38–39). Both the *tallit* and *tzitzit* are representative of God's name and all His commands.

FAITH CHECK

Wherever Jesus went, people laid the sick in His path and begged Him that they might touch the hem of His garment (Mark 6:56). The people that others condemned, Jesus made clean. When we call upon His name in faith, we touch the hem of Jesus's garment, and like the woman with the issue of blood, we are made whole.

A day that
is hemmed in
prayer will not
come unraveled.

Money Troubles

From whom do the kings of the earth take customs or taxes?
—MATTHEW 17:25 NKJV

There's a fear like no other—the kind of fear that keeps you up at night, grips your heart, and brings on panic. When your bills add up to more than you earn and your credit cards are maxed out, a special kind of anxiety sets in. *How am I going to pay the rent and the car note? How am I going to feed my family and take care of their needs? Lord Jesus, please help me!* Simon Peter was concerned about how he was going to pay the temple tax at Capernaum. But before he could talk to the Master about it, Jesus addressed the matter. He gave Peter instructions on what to do. "Go to the sea, cast in a hook, and take the fish that comes up first. And when you have opened its mouth, you will find a piece of money; take that and give it to them for Me and you" (Matthew 17:27 NKJV). God knows what we have need of before we ask. He wants to provide for us, but we need to come to Him. His Word says that we have not because we ask not.

FAITH CHECK

God can manifest gold coins from a fish's mouth to pay a tax, or provide cruets of oil and flour that replenish every day for a drought-starved family (I Kings 17:16), or multiply loaves and fishes to feed a tired, hungry crowd of five thousand (Matthew 14:13–21), or rain down manna from the sky daily for forty years to feed a nation (Exodus 16). He hears your cry! He knows your hardship and your circumstance and will provide for you in ways you cannot even imagine.

God will always provide, but His provision might look different than what you had in mind.

Not as It Seems

These people honor me with their lips,
but their hearts are far from me.
—MATTHEW 15:8 NIV

Have you ever visited an old western ghost town? As your eye follows the tangled tumbleweeds bouncing through the deserted streets, you'll likely notice the dilapidated storefronts. Once tall and elaborately decorated, the buildings appeared grand in size from the outside. But the actual buildings behind the imposing and decorative façades were half the size. The word "façade" comes from the Italian *facciata,* meaning "face." Some people live their life like those storefronts. They gussy up their exterior— the face they show to the world either through physical appearance, clothing, jewelry, cars, or houses—to make themselves look more important. Still others put on a spiritual façade. *My life is perfect. I don't need anyone to pray for me, but I'll pray for* you. There is pride and boastfulness in that attitude, and an insinuation that they think they're more sanctified and spiritual than everyone else. Sadly, in the world, a façade actually succeeds. People are easily swayed by fancy storefronts and inviting exteriors.

FAITH CHECK

God is not fooled by facades or swayed by fancy words. He sees right through it all. However, it is easy for us to fool one another. Salt looks like sugar from a distance. People have always been able to fool other people, but no one ever succeeds in deceiving God. Those who are wise confess their wrongs to God, but fools try to defend them.

When God measures
man, He puts the
measuring tape
around his heart,
not his head.

Cheese Straws

INGREDIENTS:

- 2 cups shredded sharp cheddar cheese
- 1 cup (two sticks) softened butter
- 2 cups self-rising flour
- ¼ teaspoon cayenne pepper
- ¼ teaspoon smoked paprika
- ¼ teaspoon Kosher salt
- Dash of garlic powder

DIRECTIONS:

1. Sift flour, cayenne and salt together and set aside.

2. Cream together the butter and cheese in an electric mixer. At low speed, add the flour mixture slowly and continue to beat for five minutes until creamy. Scrape down sides of bowl several times.

3. Spread a cookie sheet with parchment paper or use a silicone mat. Fill a cookie press with a star tip and pipe 3-inch-long ribbons onto the cookie sheet. Be sure to leave about one-half to one full inch between them.

4. Bake 10–15 minutes until lightly browned. Cool on racks. Yields five dozen cheese straws.

Age is not important unless you're a cheese.

—HELEN HAYES,
AMERICAN ACTRESS

Written in the Sand

Jesus said to her, "...Has no one condemned you?"
She said, "No one, LORD." And Jesus said, "Neither
do I condemn you; go and sin no more."
—JOHN 8:10-11 ESV

Rough hands pushed the frightened woman by the shoulders through a crowd of people. She was thrown in front of Jesus. "Teacher, this woman was caught in adultery." The scribes and Pharisees were gleeful. They had hatched a clever plot to accuse Jesus. If He said, "Let her go," He would have been guilty of breaking Mosaic law. If He agreed with stoning, the penalty for adultery under the law, he would be guilty of breaking Roman law because the Romans had made it illegal to execute people for religious offenses. However, Jesus did something curious. He ignored their words, stooped down, and began writing diligently in the sand with His finger. Some commentators suggest that He wrote their specific sins next to their names. The accusers continued calling for an answer, so Jesus stood and said, "He who is without sin among you, let him throw a stone at her first" (John 8:7 NKJV). One by one, the men left.

FAITH CHECK

The scribes and Pharisees could easily see the sin in others but were blind to their own sins. God carved the Ten Commandments with His finger onto stone tablets. But Jesus writes our sins in the sand because He paid the price for our sins with His own life. When we see our sinfulness before God and repent, the wind carries the record of our sins away forever.

Heaven will be the perfection we've always longed for. All the things that made Earth unlovely and tragic will be absent in heaven.

—BILLY GRAHAM

Playing Possum

These things I have spoken to you,
that in Me you may have peace.
— JOHN 16:33 NKJV

Opossum mamas often carry their entire litter on their backs. Sometimes we carry our burdens that way too, and we've been hauling them around so long, they don't even seem to be that heavy. We lumber along telling ourselves, "These problems are my cross to bear on this earth." But is that true? Jesus provides the answer. He said, "In this world you will have tribulation; but be of good cheer, I have overcome the world" (John 16:33 NKJV). We overcome our problems through praying God's Word over our situations.

When opossums are scared or under attack, they fall over in a dead faint. Poke them with a stick, and they look deader than a sack of rocks. You go to the garage for a shovel, scratching your head and thinking, *Why did that thing die? And what am I going to do with that smelly dead possum?* By the time you return, it's gone. Is the animal capable of hoodwinking you? Research suggests that the animals suffer a kind of nervous collapse when danger approaches because they are not really equipped to fight.

FAITH CHECK

Sometimes you go after the devil in prayer and as soon as you start praying, the problem seems to disappear. "God did it!" you figure. "He answered my prayers." But don't be fooled. God is answering your prayers, but sometimes the devil is "playing possum" with you. You'll soon realize that the problem is still very much alive and operating against you. So, keep praying!

There are no
crown-wearers in
heaven who were
not cross-bearers
here below.

—CHARLES SPURGEON

Joanna

And the twelve were with him, and also some women
who had been healed of evil spirits and infirmities:
Mary, called Magdalene...and Joanna, the wife of Chuza.
—LUKE 8:1-3 ESV

Joanna is one of many women who followed Jesus.
A member of the upper class, Joanna was the wife
of Chuza, the house-steward of Herod the Tetrarch
(Matthew 20:8). Luke specifically mentions the women
who followed Christ along with the disciples. To
modern sensibilities this does not seem odd; however,
in that day, rabbis usually refused to teach women. The
name Joanna means "Jehovah hath shown favor," and
she and her influential husband were forever grateful
that Jesus had shown her favor and healed her. Chuza,
Joanna, and other believers who worked for Herod
had great favor as they shared and ministered in the
Tetrarch's palace. Joanna not only followed Christ, she
delighted in ministering to Jesus out of her substance
and wealth, even arranging for places He could stay as
He and His followers traveled from town to town.

FAITH CHECK

Heartbroken, Joanna watched her Savior suffer and
die on the cross. She and the other women followed
along and took note of where the tomb was so they
could return after the Passover to anoint His body. But
when they returned with perfumed oils and spices,
they were met instead by angels who told them, "He is
not here, but risen!" (Matthew 28:6). The women who
followed after Jesus became the first to announce His
resurrection.

If you look at the world, you'll be distressed. If you look within, you'll be depressed. But if you look at Christ, you'll be at rest.

— CORRIE TEN BOOM

The Exception

I want to remind you that the LORD at one time
delivered His people out of Egypt, but later
destroyed those who did not believe.
—JUDE 1:5 NIV

Do you know for certain that you are going to heaven?
Or are you merely hoping to? Some people picture
a heavenly scoreboard where good deeds cancel out bad
ones. If you can somehow manage to keep ahead of your
sins, you'll squeeze past the gate. "Well, I cheated on
my taxes, but I held a door open for an elderly woman.
I called in sick to work so I could go to a sporting event,
but I volunteered the next week at an animal shelter."
Balances out, right? There is no heavenly scoreboard,
but there is a "Book of Life" (Revelation 20:15), and if
your name is not written in it, you won't even come close
to the gates of heaven. The Israelites were delivered by
God's mighty hand, yet those who refused to adhere
to, trust in, and rely on Him were destroyed. Not one
of them entered the Promised Land. In the great flood,
only faithful Noah and his family—eight souls—were
saved (Genesis 6:18). Only Lot and his family were
saved out of Sodom and Gomorrah (Genesis 19:14).

FAITH CHECK

You are either a Christ-follower, or you are not. You
are either covered in the blood of Jesus or stained by
sin. Heaven is open to saints and closed to sinners.
There are no exceptions, but all who repent and come
to Christ are accepted.

I have had to make a cross of two logs, and lie down on it, to show the Indians what it means to crucify a man.

—JIM ELLIOT

To Have and to Hold

By wisdom a house is built, and by understanding
it is established; by knowledge the rooms are
filled with all precious and pleasant riches.
—PROVERBS 24:3-4 ESV

Honeymooning in an exotic, romantic place is like living a fairy tale. But married life is not the glamorous union of two souls we imagine. Life gets real after couples settle back into a normal life and realize that their spouse isn't perfect. Who is perfect, though? Cinderella probably exchanged her glass slippers for fuzzy slippers soon after saying "I do." Prince Charming likely watched jousting on TV all day and developed a paunch belly. And you know that Sleeping Beauty didn't get *any* sleep after she had kids. When there are children, there's less time to cultivate that special marital relationship. Couples are too busy changing diapers, wiping snotty little noses, and tying a child's wet shoelace, and wondering why that shoelace is wet when it's not even raining outside. Let's face it, the marriage relationship is a work-in-progress that takes a lifetime to establish. The early years of marriage are difficult but more passionate, and the latter years are easier but are less about passion and more about loving companionship.

FAITH CHECK

Marriage is a Godly covenant, which means that God is in the relationship with both of you. He binds you together and unto Himself and will help you overcome the troubles that invariably challenge your life together. "So they are no longer two, but one flesh. Therefore what God has joined together, let no one separate" (Matthew 19:6 NIV).

If you're wrong and you shut up, you're wise. If you're right and you shut up, you're married.

True Superheroes

> For I have been a Nazirite to God from my mother's
> womb. If I am shaven, then my strength will leave me,
> and I shall become weak, and be like any other man."
> —JUDGES 16:17 NKJV

Samson was many things: a wise judge of Israel, a devout Nazirite from womb to tomb, a legendary one-man army, and a guy who fell for the wrong kind of women. Biblical accounts of Samson's feats of strength lead us to believe he was a juiced-up body builder who could beat down any opponent. Samson did not cut his hair, drink wine, vinegar, or anything intoxicating, or even eat grapes or raisins, and God gave Samson superhuman strength. He slaughtered an entire army of one thousand Philistines with the jawbone of an ass, and took down a lion with his bare hands. But did he look the part? Maybe not. Delilah, the curvaceous weapon whom the Philistines used to capture him, repeatedly begged to know the secret of his strength. "Please tell me where your strength lies" (Judges 16:6 ESV). Why would she ask the question if the answer was obvious? Did Samson look like a rippled-ab warrior or like a regular guy?

FAITH CHECK

Samson was the twelfth and final judge and deliverer sent to Israel, a nation spiraling downward in rebellion against God. He was a supernatural superhero of God. But so are we. Believers don't wear capes, but we are filled with the Holy Spirit and with the power to move mountains!

An affection which is not inspired by the Lord will soon be transformed into lust. Samson is not alone in the history of man in failing in this regard. Delilah is still cutting the hair of man today!

—WATCHMAN NEE

The Power of Prayer

*For the word of the cross is folly to those who are perishing,
but to us who are being saved it is the power of God.*
—I CORINTHIANS 1:18 ESV

What does it mean to put on the whole armor of God? Are we supposed to dress like Knights of the Round Table? In Ephesians 6:13–17 Christian combat basics compares our preparation as soldiers of Christ to the complete suit of armor that a heavily armed Roman soldier wore in the first century. "Loins girded with truth" means basically rolling up your sleeves to fight. The "breastplate of righteousness" means that our faith matches our actions and obedience to God. "Feet shod with the preparation of the gospel of peace" is our willingness to share the gospel with whomever God puts in our path. The "shield of faith to quench all the fiery darts" implies that your reputation as a believer goes out before you just as a shield is held out in front of you. Be true to God and His Word in every thought, deed, and action. The "helmet of salvation" was the last piece of armor a soldier put on but the most important because it protected the brain. Believers must renew and protect their minds from sin, doubt, corruption, and compromise. And finally, we take up "the sword of the spirit," which is the Word of God, our greatest weapon of all.

FAITH CHECK

When we put on the armor of God, we put on the Lord Jesus Christ (Romans 13:14). Satan knows he no longer has any hold on believers, but the greatest tool in his toolbox is the fact that most of us don't know it (Romans 8:2). The first step on the way to victory is to recognize the enemy. "There can be no victory where there is no combat" (Richard Sibbes).

You never know how big a threat you are to the enemy until you start doing something for God.

Gulliver's Travels

Ye are of God, little children, and have
overcome them: because greater is he that is
in you, than he that is in the world.
—I JOHN 4:4 KJV

The fictional character Lemuel Gulliver was shipwrecked on the island of Lilliput, but managed to swim safely to shore. Exhausted, he fell asleep on the grass and woke up to find himself tethered to the ground by numerous tiny ropes stretched across his body and limbs. Gulliver was subdued by Lilliputians, little people no more than six inches tall! To his amazement, Gulliver discovered that he was shipwrecked in a strange land, a giant on an island of diminutive folk. Sometimes we are overwhelmed by so many problems that we feel like we are as tied-down and helpless as Gulliver. Though Gulliver didn't realize his situation at first, he was a giant being held captive in a land of tiny people. All he ever had to do was sit up, and the teeny ropes that held him down would pop and snap right off. And if he stood up on his feet, he would be as tall as the Statue of Liberty to the people below.

FAITH CHECK

The enemy sends his minions against believers to cause a multitude of problems that make us feel helpless and unable to move. But the truth is, we are spiritual giants in a world of Lilliputian-sized troublemakers. God has equipped us with supernatural power in His Word, the Bible. He resides in the heart of every believer and has given us power and authority to overcome the world. "Behold, I give you the authority to trample on serpents and scorpions, and over all the power of the enemy, and nothing shall by any means hurt you" (Luke 10:19 NKJV).

Vision is the art of seeing what is invisible to others.

—JONATHAN SWIFT

Breakfast Prayer

Lord Jesus, we thank You for the first meal of this new day. May it bring good nourishment to our bodies. Please bless our family with a wealth of health, and keep us all safe and secure. We pray that You will teach us, lead us, and guide us to whatever or whomever is on Your agenda this morning, not ours. For it is written, *"In Him we live and move and have our being..." Acts 17:28 ESV*. We worship You and give You praise! Amen.

Lunchtime Prayer

Abba Father, we pray for your provision and protection as we go out into the world to work, to go to school, to travel, and to go about every normal activity we must accomplish during the day. Thank You for covering us under the shadow of Your wings, Lord God. Please grow our faith and resolve, that we may live righteous lives and turn towards You for our every need as our Source and strength. Our hope and our trust is in You Lord. *"Thou shalt not be afraid for the terror by night, nor for the arrow that flies by day; nor for the pestilence that walks in darkness; nor for the destruction that lays waste at noonday" Psalm 91 NKJV*. Amen.